Praise for *Revea*

"This is a book full of wisdom. It's sh_____ _____ _____ __ ____ ____
challenge and comfort you. It may surface your anxieties, but by the end you
will feel optimism for the possibilities that lie ahead. Combining the transition
expertise of Leslie and Mark with the experiences of peers, it provides practical
and actionable advice on how to navigate an intensely personal process. It's a
book that I can revisit to assess my progress in establishing each new season."

> – **Lucien Alziari**, EVP and CHRO, Prudential Financial, Inc.

"Leslie, Mark, and their amazing MyNextSeason team have successfully guided
numerous executives through the turbulent transition from a demanding
corporate career to finding new purpose and joy in the next phase of life. I
personally benefited from MyNextSeason's thoughtful, deliberate process for
charting a new path as described/demonstrated by this book's enlightening
personal journey stories. This book provides invaluable insights and clarity
for anyone looking to enjoy a rewarding and meaningful life post-retirement,
focusing on those you like and respect, things you enjoy and are stimulated by,
and on making your long-lasting impact."

> – **Raanan Horowitz**, Former President and CEO, Elbit America
> Board Member of Institute for Defense Analyses, Business Executives
> for National Security, and Parry Labs

"This book is an insightful, uplifting guide for anyone navigating a transition.
Through powerful stories and practical advice, you'll come away with step-by-
step guidance and a deeper sense of connection—a reminder that you're not
alone on this journey. You'll leave with a profound sense of optimism for what's
ahead, encouraging you to embrace your Next Season with confidence and hope."

> – **Michael Fraccaro**, Chief People Officer, Mastercard

"This body of work is brilliant! It provides the roadmap to plan your Next Season. It
is a brilliant collection of wisdom and the formula to plan your future Next Season."

> – **Kevin Silva**, Former Global EVP & CHRO, Voya
> Former Chair, Board of Trustees, New York Institute of Technology

"A powerful, practical read for those who wonder if their private fears and
anxiety about their transition is unique. Thank you to the many leaders who so
transparently share their struggles and journey in this book!"

> – **Mike D'Ambrose**, Former CHRO, Citigroup, First Data, ADM, Boeing
> Former CEO, Shadow Broadcast Services
> Former COO, Westwood One

"*MyNextSeason (MNS) never disappoints!* Revealing Your Next Season *is another amazing resource that includes vulnerable and heartfelt moments of those who transitioned from decades of time spent climbing the corporate ladder to moving to their personal areas of interest. The resources MNS offers are thought-provoking and practical. A hearty thanks to Leslie and Mark for another "home run!" This is a valuable book for those who are up to bat (preparing to retire), running toward next base (in process of retirement) or already slid into home plate (retired)!"*

– **Dionne Wallace Oakley**, SVP & CHRO, Freddie Mac
Shapes for You, LLC, Founder

"*This book provides invaluable advice and perspective for anyone preparing for and going through a life transition. Being aware, intentional, and authentic in making decisions during this time can lead to a richness of life that goes beyond the experiences of the corporate world. Reading this book and thoughtfully completing the tools provided can be life-changing and will provide personal insights leading to a truly purposeful and intentional Next Season.*"

– **Kim Tillotson Fleming,** Vice Chair, Baird Private Wealth
Management

"*The most astute companies understand that the best gift they can provide to their departing executives is the tailored transition services offered by MyNextSeason. While retirement parties and gifts provide a memorable way to encompass a lifetime of achievements, MyNextSeason's transition services offer a much more important mission: how to ensure that executives understand their intrinsic worth outside of the corporate structure. That mind-shift change is a vital step to fully realizing your own self-worth in your Next Season. I can speak from my own personal experience as to how valuable the personal coaching and materials from MyNextSeason were to me as I went through my own retirement experience! My coach encouraged me to dig deep, think differently about my future, and created an environment where I felt safe to share my dreams and concerns. I encourage senior executives to read this book and heed the advice!*"

– **Sharon Daley,** Former Operating Partner, Blackstone
Former VP of HR, GE Corporate | Advisor Board, GE Women's Network

"*Congratulations and thank you to Leslie and Mark on their ten-year anniversary of founding MyNextSeason! While there is uniqueness in everyone's individual retirement situation,* Revealing Your Next Season *beautifully captures the collective wisdom of the retirement experience and then offers the reader tangible insights into successfully navigating their own distinctive Next Season. No need to be a pioneer when you can learn from the best in enhancing the joy of your forward path!*"

– **Brian M. McNeill**, Chairman, President & CEO, TouchPoint, Inc.

"Braksick and Linsz have created an invaluable guide for anyone navigating career transitions. With empathy, wisdom, and actionable strategies, they help leaders unlock new levels of possibility and purpose. This book offers the clarity and insight needed to make your Next Season your best yet. I only wish that I had possessed this resource earlier in my own journey—it's a roadmap to living a life of joy, impact, and meaning."

> – **Eva Sage-Gavin**, Advisor & Former Senior Managing Director of Talent & Organization/Human Potential, Accenture | Advisory Councils, Stanford University's Clayman Institute for Gender Research and Stanford Center on Longevity | Board Member, Innovation Resource Center for Human Resources | Co-Chair, Women Corporate Directors, Bay Area Chapter

"I imagine my Next Season to be one of discovery, purpose, joy, and renewal. Having a clear plan will allow me to meet the change with optimism and meaning. Leslie and Mark offer great advice and examples of how to reveal the possibilities that lie ahead!"

> – **Glenda McNeal**, Chief Partner Officer, American Express

"Your Next Season may be your very best with careful planning. The first critical step is "Pause for Discernment" before leaping ahead. With the advice and tools provided by Leslie Braksick and Mark Linsz, navigation through the steps and decision-making is made much easier and more successful."

> – **Jim Unruh**, Founding Principal, Alerion Capital Group, LLC

"Revealing Your Next Season is an invaluable roadmap for executives planning or navigating their next act. Leslie and Mark share a decade of insights through compelling stories of leaders who successfully transitioned to fulfilling Next Seasons."

> – **Jack Ryan**, Senior Advisor, Rockefeller Capital Management

"Working with my MyNextSeason Advisor helped me prepare for a successful transition from a 30+ year career in financial services. I was able to retire on my own terms, with optimism about the future and a roadmap to guide the decisions about how to spend my time in this next chapter."

> – **Titi Cole** (Retired), C-Suite Financial Services Leader Independent Board Director

"Throughout my decades-long career as an HR professional and CHRO, I had the opportunity to work with some incredible leaders who delivered immense value for their organizations' stakeholders. The best leaders were not daunted by the unknown or fearful of taking big swings for their organizations, yet many struggle when it comes time to plan for all the unknowns on the other side of their corporate world and role. In Revealing Your Next Season, *Leslie Braksick and Mark Linsz provide an outline for executives who are readying themselves for their own big swing. Through a combination of structured planning advice, tools and tips, and inspirational stories of prior clients, executives can begin envisioning, planning for, and experiencing a Next Season filled with purpose, impact, and joy."*

  – **Marty Gervasi**, Former CHRO, The Hartford Financial Services Group, Inc. | Independent Director, POOLCORP

"Drs. Braksick and Innes's first book, Your Next Season, *was incredibly well-researched and presented in a way that was so useful and engaging. I absolutely LOVED it and really benefitted from the book and the overall MyNextSeason program as I transitioned to my 'rewirement,' as I called it. I gifted it to so many people during the past several years, who thanked me for helping them transition. The same will be true with* Revealing Your Next Season. *This is a must-read for anyone transitioning to whatever is next. One's spouse/partner and other family members can also benefit from the approach they take of addressing the whole person, and the positive opportunities that can lie ahead, and connecting all of those dots, since retirement can be daunting to the family as well. The vignettes by others who have already been on this journey are filled with GEMS! I've re-read the first book numerous times with lots of underlining and am sure we will all do the same with* Revealing Your Next Season. *Well done!"*

  – **Doria Camaraza** (Retired), SVP/General Manager, American Express

"What a wonderful collection of sage advice for executives transitioning from warp-speed lifestyles and slammed calendars to more peaceful lives grounded in greater purpose. Dr. Braksick and Mark Linsz give us a compelling reminder that it is okay to press the "pause" button and take some time to plan for a Next Season not orchestrated by the world around us, but rather shaped by our own gifts, aspirations, and imaginations . . . and, or course, a few whispers from above."

  – **Mike Sharp** (Retired), Corporate Real Estate Executive, Bank of America | Founder & Owner, Lighthouse Consulting Corporation

"I have read your new book, and it's incredibly wonderful in many ways. Using the client's and advisor's "own words" is a mark of genius and speaks the truth of the overall impact of the MyNextSeason journey. Some profound, many salient words and phrases sprinkled throughout these chapters tell the stories of anguish, turmoil, discovery, relief, and celebration. These are real-life phases both the client and advisor have traversed. Thank you for bringing us all together to help find our greater purpose."

– **Vanessa J. Castagna**, Former SVP of Merchandising, Wal-Mart & Target
Former Chairwoman, Mervyn's Department Stores
Former CEO and Chairwoman, JCPenney Stores, Catalogue, and Internet
Board of Trustees, Board Executive Committee, Audit and Enterprise Risk
Committee (Chair), Purdue University

"I was introduced to the MyNextSeason team when my firm, Deloitte Canada, engaged them to coach and provide advice to partners who are within 5 years of retirement. I benefited greatly from their advice and methodical way to chart a path forward along with my wife, planning the next phase(s) of life post-Deloitte. I also was very fortunate to benefit from 1:1 chats and advice with Mark Linsz, whom I now consider a personal friend, exploring many common areas of interest, and building on his personal and professional experience. I found this new book, with the personal stories and hands-on advice and almost step-by-step guidance, to be the most practical book on preparing professionals and executives for retirement. Once I started reading, I couldn't stop, completing it in one long weekend. I highly recommend this book and the MyNextSeason team to all my colleagues at Deloitte and others in the same profession."

– **Adel Melek**, Global Vice Chair, Deloitte

"We recommend this book highly to anyone considering how best to navigate the varied and complex stages of life. Leslie and Mark provide a roadmap, filled with content that is inspiring, thoughtful, interesting, and grounded in common sense—with lessons shared by an extraordinary and talented group of people who have found unique purpose in their Next Seasons."

– **Alan and Carol Kelly,** Entrepreneurs and philanthropists.
Alan is retired VP, ExxonMobil Corporation, and retired President, ExxonMobil Downstream Marketing.

"Each individual's approach to, and success with, the transition from corporate life to that of a retired executive is, indeed, unique. Some seem to do it effortlessly, while others struggle and never find their way. This book recognizes that wide variation, and with many testimonials from those who have faced and made the transition, it provides structure and many helpful suggestions to plan and achieve the retirement that is right for you."

> – **David Clair** (Retired), President, Exxon Research & Engineering

"Revealing Your Next Season *provides a holistic approach in serving an important unmet need. I had a successful transition to my Next Season by following the tenets of this book—clarity of purpose, health, and companionship.*"

> – **Dee Mellor** (Retired), Officer, General Electric Company

"*An excellent guide for executives transitioning into retirement. While the authors have used their extensive experience and interviews to focus on senior executives, I believe this book is an appropriate guide for many non-executives approaching retirement.*"

> – **Michael Ramage** (Retired), EVP, ExxonMobil Research & Engineering Company

"*To the best of my knowledge, this book is a first. It thoroughly addresses the important subject of how to make your transition from a life of running hard every day to one of using your gifts and experience in a way that is purposeful and fulfilling. It explains the process, provides real-life examples, and includes tools to guide you and your spouse/partner on the journey.*"

> – **Frank Berardi** (Retired), Director of Employee Development,
> The Allstate Corporation
> Former Executive Coach at ALULA
> Founder & Coach, Callahan Group

"*A great guide for the retiring executive, this book provides a wonderful path through the transition from retirement to a Next Season. It explores the thoughts and feelings that often accompany retirement and the uncertainty beyond. It is well-written, complete with great advice, thoughts from many executives who have blazed the trail already, and practical tips on how to plan and execute the process.*"

> – **Richard Downen** (Retired), Executive, Bank of America
> Vice Chairman, Community Board of Directors, Hampton Hall
> Chairman, Golf Board of Directors, Hampton Hall

© 2024 MyNextSeason

Revealing Your Next Season
ISBN: 979-8-3424372-5-7 (print)
ISBN: 979-8-89589-174-2 (ebook)

For permission to use any portion of this book, please email info@mynextseason.com or contact MyNextSeason, 429 East Blvd., Charlotte, NC 28203.

Library of Congress Cataloging-in-Publication Data

Braksick, Leslie W.

Linsz, Mark D.

New title and ISBN #

1. Retirement
2. Executives
3. Career Transition
4. Coaching
5. Life Transition
6. Career Planning
7. Finding Purpose

Book Design: Scattaregia Design

First edition published 2024 by MyNextSeason

Printed in the United States of America

Revealing Your Next Season

Reflections on 10 Years of Supporting Leaders Transitioning from Intense Careers to Fulfilling Next Seasons

Contents

Dedication

For **Steve Simon** and **Liam McGee**, whose Next Seasons were cut too short.

For the thousands of MyNextSeason clients, who have been our life's work during our first decade as a company. Thank you for trusting us, thank you for teaching us, and thank you for inspiring us by your purposeful Next Seasons. This book was possible because of you.

To Everything There Is a Season

To everything there is a season,
and a time to every purpose under heaven:

a time to be born and a time to die, a time to plant and a time to uproot,
a time to kill and a time to heal,

a time to tear down and a time to build, a time to weep and a time to laugh,

a time to mourn and a time to dance,

a time to scatter stones and a time to gather them,

a time to embrace and a time to refrain from embracing, a time to search
and a time to give up,

a time to keep and a time to throw away, a time to tear and a time to mend,

a time to be silent and a time to speak, a time to love and a time to hate,

a time for war and a time for peace.

What do workers gain from their toil? I have seen the burden God has laid on
the human race.

He has made everything beautiful in its time. He has also set eternity in
the human heart; yet no one can fathom what God has done from beginning
to end.

I know that there is nothing better for people than to be happy and to
do good while they live.

That each of them may eat and drink, and find satisfaction in all their toil—
this is the gift of God.

I know that everything God does will endure forever; nothing can be added
to it and nothing taken from it.

> — *Ecclesiastes 3:1–14*
> *from the King James Version and the New International Version*

Foreword

WHEN LESLIE BRAKSICK asked me to write the Foreword to her 2017 book, *Your Next Season*, I was both honored and eager to contribute my thoughts. Leslie and I go back a long way. I first met her in 2008 when she was interviewing GE chairman and CEO Jeff Immelt for another book she was writing at the time, *Preparing CEOs for Success: What I Wish I Knew.*

Based on those early conversations, we invited Leslie and her colleague Bill Innes to work with some of our leaders as executive coaches. Leslie created her own Next Season in 2014 when, together with Mark Linsz, they started their new company, MyNextSeason. We immediately retained Leslie and her team as trusted advisors at GE, helping our retired executives contemplate their next act after retirement.

Fast-forward to 2024. In the decades that I've known Leslie, we have had hours, days, and even weeks of time working together, traveling together, talking together, and building a deep friendship. In many ways, the story of our relationship is the story of this book. It speaks to transitions, opportunities, and relationships. Our relationship is built on an incredible foundation and shared belief system. We both have an optimistic view of leadership. We both believe that the best leaders have a knack for seeing around corners, that they have an intense curiosity, and they are energized by change and see potential in the unknown.

But we have also come to see and experience that even incredible leaders like these don't always know how to transition from their impactful and acclaimed careers to their next chapter. With *Revealing Your Next Season*, Leslie and Mark have taken the guesswork out of this transition to life's proverbial third act. If you are approaching retirement or have already retired, this book is for you.

Retirement is a significant change. Change, ultimately, is a matter of learning and adapting. It often requires a mindset shift. You are likely more prepared than you realize.

Think of the finely honed capabilities you have developed through your career: your ability to influence, to make tough calls, to rally a team around a vision, to spot talent, and help others rise higher. With this incredible foundation, I encourage you to think broadly and deeply about what you may yet achieve. Use this book as your guide. The world needs your capabilities now more than ever.

The essence of this book, and of success in your Next Season, is determining what is next for *you*. You will create that success with different "stakeholders" now—family, friends, yourself—and you will do it in a whole new way. If that feels a little uncomfortable and open-ended, dive into this book as an investment in your future.

Luckily for you, you have the research, perspective, and knowledge of Leslie, Mark, and their team. Together with the insights of many who have walked this road already, Leslie and Mark will help you determine where your deep, perhaps forgotten passions might lead.

Revealing Your Next Season is an investment in a future you may not yet have imagined for yourself, but one that awaits you with open arms and untold promise. *Carpe diem!*

Susan P. Peters
Hilton Head, South Carolina
August 2024

....

Susan P. Peters was the Senior Vice President of Human Resources for General Electric Company and their global workforce of over 300,000 at the time of her retirement in 2018. From 2007 to 2013 she served as GE's Vice President of Executive Development and Chief Learning Officer. Susan currently sits on two public boards and one nonprofit charity-focused board. She is especially appreciative of the time she gets to spend with family (including her two granddaughters) and friends. She is a proud product of the influence on her retirement of Leslie Braksick and this book.

Advice from a Fellow Journeyman

RETIREMENT FROM A FULL-ON corporate career is one of the most dramatic events of your life—and, in most cases, the least planned-for. Your Next Season cannot be thought of as just another job to add to your resume. It is vastly different! It is a whole new set of experiences and challenges. You might assume that your work career has fully prepared you to handle retirement, but that's just not so. Fortunately, this book presents a clear guide as you enter this unique phase of your life.

Given that we identify with our career, title, and position, a poorly planned retirement can leave you adrift, without a clear purpose, role, or definition. And given that we all are products of our past experiences, you might not anticipate that your Next Season could in fact be your most glorious. As your Next Season inevitably approaches, the big question you face is: will it be a parade of ongoing unplanned, unpredictable, and random events, or will it be a life of joy, meaning, and fulfillment?

Many fear this next chapter in life because it may be unknown and so very different from your seasons that preceded it. Yet, with thoughtful planning and reflection, your Next Season could be your most fulfilling. Financial planning is sometimes advertised as the singular solution to a productive next season, yet in fact wealth is only a small portion of it. You can enter your Next Season with financial security, yet still lack fulfilling direction, purpose, and joy.

Our past experiences rarely prepare us to outline our Next Season. Thus, learning from the experiences of our predecessors is what enables and encourages us to enjoy a high-quality Next Season. Only naivete would lead us to believe that we can enter this next phase knowing all the answers.

When you choose a career, defining what gives you joy, peace, meaning, and purpose rarely tops your list of criteria. Yet these considerations need to top your list of building blocks for your Next Season. Joy, peace, meaning, and purpose now become your key criteria to contemplate, discover, and build your new, different future.

Is your Next Season something that will just happen to you? Or will you craft it and make it work? You cannot afford to enter your Next Season ill-prepared. There is a protocol for enjoying a secure and meaningful Next Season, and it is presented in this must-read book. Embrace it all!

Kevin Silva
New York, New York
September, 2024

. . . .

Kevin Silva was the Executive Vice President and Chief Human Resource Officer at Voya Financial, a position he held for approximately 12 years. Prior to that, Kevin held senior Executive roles at Mastercard, Merrill Lynch, MBIA, Argo, and PepsiCo. He was named an Executive Mentor of the Year by the 30% Club for successfully mentoring many emerging executives in their careers over recent years. He has helped to build public company Boards and C-suite executive teams. He has served as Chairman of the Board of Trustees of the New York Institute of Technology. His master's degree from NYU is in Psychology and he has successfully assisted countless executives in career transitions at each of his companies.

1

Prelude: Carpe Diem!

Embrace the gift of transitions

During our careers, we came to appreciate how incredibly difficult—and lonely—transitions can be, dramatically impacting health, emotional wellbeing, and relationships. One of the biggest transitions is retirement—which seems far away until it's not. Over the past two decades, the decision to retire, and when to do it, was increasingly shifting out of the hands of individual leaders who had been so dedicated to their companies for decades and into the hands of employers as part of strategic talent management.

Most leaders thought they'd have (more) time to plan for what they would do after their corporate careers. Even those who chose the timing of their retirement often struggled with what to do next. These leaders didn't need "outplacement help"; they needed a new purpose, a new identity, new networks, and new routines for good health. They still had so much they wanted to accomplish—with considerable runway to make it happen. Support for this pivot was not the purview of Human Resources or the companies in which people worked, and there was no organization whose mission was to provide sensitive, yet pragmatic, individualized support.

Thus, the idea for MyNextSeason was born. Ten years ago, we created our company, dedicated to making a meaningful difference, both for professionals and their organizations during times of transition.

Our vision was, and continues to be, simple but powerful—to provide a guiding light through the intricate paths of career transitions, guidance that helps people when they need it most. Our passion stems from a shared belief that navigating these pivotal moments (among the most vulnerable and important in one's life) with care, understanding, and personalized support will shape the trajectory of the rest of their lives.

MyNextSeason's success and evolution are a testament to the market's need for transition support, fueled by our dedication to providing comprehensive solutions at every stage of the career continuum.

As we look back at the myriad individuals and companies we've been privileged to serve, we feel truly honored. Our clients have entrusted us not only with their hopes and aspirations, but also their fragility, concerns, and fears. Working together, each client emerged with thoughtful, intentional plans for revealing a Next Season even more bold and rewarding than the career-intense one left behind.

That has been our greatest joy, and we have been honored to remain in touch with so many we have supported. Their photos, stories, and posts underscore the impact they are making on boards, teaching at universities, launching and impacting not-for-profits, reconnecting with family, being grandparents of the year, finally writing that book, and becoming clean consumers and exercise fanatics.

Throughout this book, you can read and be inspired by some of their individual stories, titled "Retirement Redefined."

Ten years from now, should we profile these same people, their stories would be different. Why? Because everyone has not just one, but multiple Next Seasons. Most of these stories are just about their first Next Seasons. As we stress in this book, there will be other Next Seasons . . . driven by life events, health changes, new interest areas, and environmental-political-socioeconomic factors that impact our lives. Many things can trigger a Next Season. That's what you are doing now—

developing "muscle memory" for navigating transitions that will serve you well for the rest of your life.

But this book is not just about retirement—it speaks to transitions we face throughout our careers and lives. Transitions are windows of opportunity to celebrate and capitalize on.

We present this book to help you prepare for a transition (or navigate a current one) by sharing lessons learned by our clients, and ourselves, over the past decade. It builds upon what we shared in our company's first book: *Your Next Season* (Braksick & Innes, 2017). We hope you will be inspired and reassured by the advice, stories, and choices of those who walked the path ahead of you.

We hope it will widen the aperture that leads to possibilities not previously imagined, joys not ever contemplated. As we stand at this milestone, we recommit ourselves to the values that have shaped MyNextSeason (mynextseason.com)—deep empathy, a dedication to excellence, and an unwavering belief in the transformative power of thoughtful career guidance.

To all things—there is a season. Embrace this time of transition. We will help you navigate it. To quote George Eliot: "It's never too late to be what you might have been."

Carpe Diem!

Before founding MyNextSeason . . .

Dr. Leslie Braksick spent her career as CEO of a behaviorally-based consulting firm she co-founded, leading, growing, supporting and advising leaders of our nation's biggest companies.

Mark Linsz spent his career as a corporate Treasurer and Risk Officer, leading others, and developing and delivering ambitious strategies on behalf of his former employer, Bank of America.

2

The Most Important Piece of Our Life Puzzle Is Often Neglected

What you choose to do when you conclude your main career is the most important decision of that life phase

From your earliest days, you were pushed to look decades ahead and employ elaborate financial schemes (401k, 403b, Roth IRA, HSA, Social Security) to secure income when you would eventually downshift (aka retire). To help you look ahead, planners, advisors, and HR Benefits experts ensured that you didn't leave this to chance.

Throughout your life and career, you had countless conversations about your fiscal future—planning, investing, the economy.

But the biggest future piece of your life puzzle may have been (unintentionally) ignored. How many conversations did you have about what you will do when that downshift occurs? What would you like to do with your time? How will retiring from your main career affect you and your family? What (new things) will bring you joy and purpose when you are no longer working for the company?

You amassed superpowers throughout your career, but did you ever systematically explore how you might apply them differently? Have you ever contemplated the dramatic evolution you've achieved—personally and professionally—since you began working?

Like everyone else running at your speed, you were probably too consumed to spend time on seemingly way-down-the-road concerns.

If you are in the midst of transition, or are now thinking about retirement, questions may now be coming at you like curveballs:

- How will I spend my time, really?

- What will be my identity, when I'm no longer attached to my company and role?

- How will I find my new purpose?

- Who are the people I want in my inner circle? (versus colleagues placed around me due to circumstance)

Preparing for this major life transition is deeply personal and unique to you. It's time to discern what you choose to spend your time on, with whom, where you want to live, and how you define success in your Next Season. Each of these factors requires (and deserves) thoughtful study, by both you and your life partner, for they, too, are deeply affected by all this. Unfortunately, we don't just wake up one day with an epiphany that answers these important questions.

Similarly, we don't magically acquire new relationships/connections to achieve the new possibilities we desire. Nor do most of us have existing deep and trusted friendships we are comfortable being completely vulnerable with, to help us navigate this intense period of change.

In the past decade, we at MyNextSeason have affirmed that this discernment and transition into your Next Season is greatly enabled by guided self-reflection and accessing wisdom of those who preceded you on the journey.

Once you have a clear plan, you will lean into what's next with great optimism and excitement. (But until then, it can be an incredibly destabilizing period of time.)

We have developed, tested, and continually refined a powerful methodology that gets you there. We have learned a lot in our ten years of advising, and we are excited to pass it all on—so you too will discover a Next Season that is fit-for-purpose (yours), fulfilling, honors you and those you love, and ushers in a new season of your life even more gratifying than the career you are leaving.

As Far-Sighted Leaders, Why Don't We Focus Earlier on Our Next Season?

When we are in the heat of battle, it's hard to imagine what's at the end! Our lives are consumed with calls and meetings, travel and dinners out, presentations, explanations, expense reports, budgets, and on and on. There are endless demands for your time, opinions, and decisions. It is a relentlessly *busy*, all-consuming lifestyle.

The higher you are in your organization, the more command your employer has over your non-work time and commitments. Add your family obligations, and you have a schedule that is long on obligations and short on time. It is hard, if not impossible, for leaders to commit to non-work opportunities due to their ever-shifting schedules. Even close friendships tend to have a work connection—and sadly, many of those "work friendships" change when there is no longer commonality of the workplace every day.

. . . .

After a lifetime of being part of a fast-moving machine, we cannot imagine a future without a title, a portfolio, or a primary company affiliation that tells the world who we are. *Who am I when I am no longer the admired leader of such-and-such?* It is only natural to dwell on what was rather than what will be.

The good news is: A career transition of this magnitude presents you with an opportunity to shift from a season of *gaining* personal value, to one of *giving* personal value. New possibilities are endless. The question is how to get there, how to navigate this challenging phase of life.

Should your exit come sooner than expected, or if you are not asked to stay longer, it is natural to experience disappointment and anger. After so many years of personal sacrifice, commitment, and loyalty to the company, you expect more love from your former employer, and more generosity from your exit package.

The Inspiration for MyNextSeason

STEVE, A COACHING CLIENT of Leslie's, was one of the greats. His amazing run culminated in Vice Chairmanship of a Fortune 10 company. At his retirement party, upon being offered heartfelt congratulations: "Steve, you must feel so proud of all you've achieved and your impact on our industry, which you helped shape!" Steve leaned in and shared in a stressed and vulnerable voice, "this is the worst day of my life!"

Steve had a successful 48-year marriage and a family he loved. But his life was his work. His identity was the company and his role in it. Without either, he felt lost. He desperately wanted to find purpose in his Next Season, but didn't know where to look, or how.

Steve reached out to Leslie for help. He knew he needed help figuring out what to do next—and thought perhaps she could help since she had coached him earlier in his career. Leslie was painfully aware she had no "executive career transition advisor" she could refer Steve to . . . no one who "got" why this was so hard a transition for Steve, whose day job was to help leaders like him navigate a fragile career transition. Thirteen months later, while at home alone, Steve had a massive heart attack that took his life instantly.

Steve's death not only inspired this book, but the founding of our company, MyNextSeason, dedicated to helping leaders transition from careers of intense productivity to lives of purpose, discovering their fulfilling Next Seasons.

Steve's stress and related physical health issues are not unique. It's very hard for leaders to switch gears after decades of unwavering devotion to their company. It's hard to find identity after years of having it defined through work and a job title. This is precisely why transitioning is not just flipping a switch. It is a thoughtful, planful process of discerning and discovery.

We formed MyNextSeason so the "next Steve" would have a place to go for help.

Steve needed a team of professionals who understood and could help him, and others like him, navigate this important, vulnerable time of transition, develop a plan for what to do next, and discover even greater purpose and joy.

Do concerns about "what's next," and your identity once you leave your corporate role, describe you? If so, take heart: you are not alone. You are why we wrote this book.

What Have You Always Wanted to Do?

For the first time in a long, long while, your corporate employer is no longer determining what, where, or when you do everything. So, what have you always wanted to do? Who have you always wanted to share it with? What would bring joy to your life? This is a season of possibilities and often, in retirement, the answer to these questions is much more of a family decision—which requires inclusion of your spouse/partner in the conversation.

. . . .

Liam was our first client. He transitioned from Chairman/CEO of The Hartford Financial Services Group, Inc., but terminal cancer forced him to retire long before he wanted to. Strategic executive hiring and development by his company ensured there were ready successors for his CEO role. This enabled what could have been a high-drama transition to happen with relative calm and grace. Liam entered his Next Season with profound clarity and purpose, and a desire to be as accomplished in his final season as he was in his prior ones.

Working hand-in-glove with his wife Lori, they moved their young boys to be closer to extended family. Liam secured joint faculty appointments in law and business at his alma mater and began mentoring first-time CEOs of not-for-profits. He wanted to share his life lessons and advice with those who otherwise could not access a coach with his deep experience.

Liam used to text us after those coaching sessions to say how much fun he was having—and how well-purposed he felt coaching others as they assumed greater leadership roles.

Thus, in his remaining time, Liam did what was important to him at that stage of his life. First and foremost, he spent time with his family, attending his children's events and being with them. Second, he channeled his work-focused energies by publishing his reflections, sharing them in the classroom and during coaching of his CEO mentees. The legacy from his Next Season quickly became as meaningful to him as the legacy from his decades-long corporate career.

In his memory, his wife Lori McGee wrote this thoughtful tribute.

Thoughts on leaving a lasting legacy

LEAVING A LEGACY becomes more impactful and meaningful through conversations with your spouse or partner, family members, or business partners, so your goal is achieved together.

My husband Liam embarked on his Next Season while courageously battling cancer. At MyNextSeason, Leslie helped Liam plan his legacy and continue making a difference beyond his corporate success. She advised him on teaching opportunities, documenting his valuable experience, and publishing his wisdom in the business press. Leslie was instrumental in keeping Liam's voice "alive" even after he passed.

The whole idea of "Making a Difference" fueled me to honor his legacy by living Liam's motto—Strive for Greatness—a top leadership lesson he exemplified during his career. Our family decided to partner with the National Cancer Center to launch a brain tumor research fund in his honor.

I am blessed to volunteer at that Center to assist families living with cancer throughout their journey. It brings me great peace and joy to know that I am working toward Liam's legacy of impacting others. Great strides have been made toward extending and improving quality of life for patients.

Even before his retirement, Liam and I had thoughtful, intentional discussions about leaving a lasting legacy. If we had not done this, I would have lacked clarity about next steps. Liam had already left his mark as a visionary leader in business, but now his impact is helping those challenged by cancer or adversity.

I encourage everyone to seek expert advice to further their impact in their Next Season. Perhaps your company career was a springboard to leaving an even broader legacy that might include sponsoring and tutoring underrepresented students, or mentoring neophytes in an industry with your expertise, or launching a whole new career with a social cause.

—*Lori McGee*

. . . .

Liam McGee is one of two leaders to whom this book is dedicated. Liam was Chairman/CEO of The Hartford when he retired prematurely due to brain cancer. Determined to share his life lessons, he devoted his Next Season to mentoring first-time CEOs of not-for-profits, publishing white papers on business leadership, and securing joint faculty appointments in the Colleges of Business and Law at his alma mater.

Career Transition Planning While Still in the Game

Increasingly, we come across executives who were very intentional about career choices and priorities, while still fully vested in their current roles. These individuals chose to engage in Next Season planning with great intentionality, hope, and anticipation. They've worked hard for many decades and are excited for the possibilities that await them.

We observed that these folks are deliberate about hobbies, relationships, and goals for themselves, even while still in their career roles. They anticipate their Next Seasons of discovery and good health, and are greeting the unexpected with a sense of possibility!

Kim, a former client, was Chairman/CEO of a private wealth management company she led and grew. As part of her succession planning, she sold the company to a former competitor she long admired, and she is now Vice Chair of the combined entity. Kim offers the following reflection:

> *I have found it incredibly important to engage in annual transition thinking and planning. I do a 3-day personal retreat by myself once a year, in a remote and beautiful place. I begin by reflecting backward, and then think about priorities in all different aspects of my life. That time spent is the most important of my entire year. It is so valuable to take personal time and create space to be contemplative and intentional on things such as relationships, new interests, health, etc. Putting my self-observations and goals in writing is non-negotiable. It solidifies my perspective and becomes my playbook for the year—which, of course, will likely be tweaked or revised as needed.*
>
> *As I examine this ritual, I realize that one of its most valuable aspects is gaining a strong sense of self outside the corporate world, not tied to my position or title. Through this annual process, I have discovered that my most satisfying experiences are those that have had an impact on others. This awareness, which I might not have achieved otherwise, helps ensure that I continue creating these experiences in whatever comes next in my life. And by the way—I have no intention of retiring anytime soon! It is up to me to ensure balance at every phase of my life.*

It's never too early and never too late to begin Next Season planning. Give yourself grace as you commit to begin a process that may be new to you. Be patient with yourself as you prepare to close the corporate chapter of your story and begin writing your next chapter—or your new book. This is YOUR STORY, in which you are both the author and the main character. Honor yourself by being intentional in how you write that story and what that main character does. It's never too late to pivot.

Your Next Season is brimming with possibilities. So, lean in and keep moving forward. Your best days are still ahead!

Rob Arning

Previous Role: KPMG Vice Chair and Foundation Chairman

Retirement Date: 2020

Next Season Passions:
- Dedicated Mentor & Volunteer
- Passionate Outdoorsman
- Loving Life Off the Grid!

Retiring during a pandemic

My first months of retirement were made even more uncertain because of Covid. The world was already "retiring" from day-to-day normalcy. There were very few opportunities to connect in person with clients, colleagues, and friends to reminisce and say goodbye and thank you! In some ways, it was a quiet, peaceful start to my Next Season, but I felt a void, not being able to visit with those who had meant so much to me for 37 years!

I also felt that I needed to be more thoughtful and deliberate about what was next. I was entering uncharted waters in many ways. While I had happy and exciting moments, I often wondered, "What will tomorrow really feel like?" The closest parallel is how I felt the day after my oldest child was born—everything changed, all very good and exciting, but very different. It was the same on my first day of retirement.

Should I, or shouldn't I?

In the beginning, there was a lot of exploring. I felt one way at night and a different way in the morning. Should I consult, teach, serve on boards, work part-time, or do it all again and build a business development strategy for another organization? I was presented with many great opportunities and kept several doors open I will likely revisit as I move further into retirement. It's an amazing gift to have the flexibility to simply enjoy your life in whatever way you choose. I now enjoy doing what I choose, rather than what others think I should. For the first time in decades, I'm in control of my schedule, and it feels great!

Valuable validation

MyNextSeason helped me reveal what I really wanted. I nearly signed up for a few new roles until I realized they might not be the right fit. I realized I absolutely loved the complete freedom and flexibility to try different things and explore! I was never bored, and my schedule was actually too busy with fun things.

> **"**
> *I realized I absolutely loved the complete freedom and flexibility to try different things and explore!"*

I remember calling my Advisor at one point and asking, "Am I crazy? I'm really having a good time and want to enjoy it. I want to sign up for a few of the right things but leave lots of room on my calendar and see what's next." He said, "Absolutely not. It's your Next Season, and you just figured out what it's going to be." If I hadn't talked it through, I might have made decisions I would have had to unwind.

Take your time

Give it a year, at least. Put your feelers out. Initiate your conversations. Keep them alive. Don't close any doors, but avoid signing on the dotted line too often or too early, because you won't feel the same way a year after you retire as you did on the first day!

No structure, no regrets

I have no sense that I should have continued working full-time. I was several months into retirement when it became apparent that I had this passion to just enjoy every day and pursue personal interests I never had time for. I don't want a fully booked calendar. I absolutely love the freedom to wander. I just booked trips to a classic car show and a boat show a month later. No conflicts on my calendar!

Finding new joy in giving back

I represented KPMG in many philanthropic efforts throughout my career. Now, I'm enjoying giving back on a more personal level through philanthropy, coaching, and mentoring. I remain very active with the American Cancer Society, the finance committee at my church, and my alma mater, Long Island University. Those organizations bring issues to the table that I can really impact. I also can support my wife and her interests, most notably her effort to address hunger and homelessness on Long Island. Now I can be there for her, as she was for me during my time at KPMG.

The gift that keeps giving

It's a great gift to retire. I loved my career, the friends I made, the clients I served, and the experiences I had. But 80% or more of everything about me went to KPMG for 37 years. To now redirect 80% of who I am to other priorities and interests is a great feeling of freedom, happiness, and satisfaction. Can you remember the summer after Senior year of high school? It's like that, but it doesn't end! It's all about being with your friends and family, doing things important to you, laughing, and enjoying each day. It feels like endless summer!

3

Why Are Career Transitions So Hard?

It's not about endings, but beginnings

Many books have been written about how to retire success-fully. But with young-in-age and young-in-life leaders transitioning out of companies today, it is no longer just about retirement, but more broadly about transitioning to what's next.

Transitions are not about endings, but beginnings. And the least-mentioned, yet most important part, is the act of transition itself: bridging from your current state to your future state—and ensuring it happens well.

Major Career Transitions Are Just Plain Hard, for Good Reasons

In retirement or any transition, there is generally more uncertainty than clarity about what's next, more questions than answers. There is a loss of identity, and for many, a loss of purpose. The known and past were familiar and comfort-able (even if parts of it were unpleasant or unfun). But at least we knew what to expect, and we knew who we would be navigating with.

Our professions and careers come to define us. It's how we are known in our communities and the currency we use to get things done. It's the ticket to enter conversations and situations of importance. It's the place we feel most comfortable, most impactful, most useful. On our best days, it's how we remind ourselves that we are worthy, important, and that what we do matters. And on our worst days, it kicks our butt and prompts us to try again, differently, better, somehow changed. In either case, it is "work" that sits at the center and makes us who we are. It is the beast we feed. No wonder we feel such a jolt and intense loss when it comes to an end!

One of our clients, Brian, retired from a key operating leadership role when his company did a mega-merger. Directors and the new CEO urged Brian to accept a major job in the combined entity, because he was a highly respected leader and executive. But Brian saw a new beginning: he opted to sail from the US to Australia, his home country, over many, many months, with his wife of many, many years. He shared that:

Men die young in my lineage, and I don't want to spend another day away from the person I love most in the world, doing the thing I enjoy most in the world, that will deliver me to the rest of the people I care most about in the world.

Transitioning to a meaningful Next Season often requires quieting outside voices that try to convince you of what you should do and letting go of any feelings of guilt or perceived obligation.

Looking forward, there will be days where you enjoy simple, unstructured time with those you care about, get lost in a novel, spend a day fly fishing, sail to Australia, or simply enjoy some fresh air and sunshine. Other days will be spent with great focus, fulfilling a personal goal. Some days will blend one into another, because they can . . . and because there is no one checking, no one keeping score. Living into your Next Season involves allowing all of those possibilities to unfold as they are meant to, and to be "okay."

Transitions that You Don't Initiate Can Really Sting

Many leaders find themselves in transition well in advance of their desires or plans. These shortened windows are creating abrupt endings for a generation of leaders who left it all on the field, making sacrifices to benefit their companies.

Transitions mandated by your employer are usually unexpected, unwelcome, and upsetting. You may experience feelings of embarrassment or humiliation in both public and private conversations, having to explain "why" and "why now." Increasingly, as companies play a stronger role in strategic talent management, senior moves are initiated according to company needs, not your wants or preferences. And even though such a move has no tie to your performance, it can often feel like a firing.

Here are some examples from our clients—

George was Chairman/CEO of a global company. With only three months' notice, the board handed George's role to his successor—a full two years before he expected to transition out. He was upset and felt disrespected after a selfless career with the company, including multiple international relocations with his family and weekly global travel and commitments. He reflected:

It felt like a death sentence. I was shocked and disappointed, with no plan in place for what to do next. I wish I had spent more time pondering and prepping for the transition. I needed to sever my emotional relationship with the company, because I disagreed with many changes they were making. I also disagreed with the views of my successor. Frankly, I needed to accept that I was no longer in control, and separate myself emotionally from actions being planned under my successor's regime. It was eating me alive. I needed to preserve myself!

I realized that I needed to focus energy on my family and personal relationships—immediately—because I had shortchanged them during my career. It became clear I could only do this by focusing on my future and not holding on to my past.

Today, George is on the other side of the transition:

I am happier than I have ever been! I thoroughly love being in charge of my own time and schedule. I have more time for my private life, children, and grandchildren. I have found purpose in my church volunteer work and the other organizations I have chosen. Achieving happiness necessitated my letting go—really letting go—and I realize now that part of what made that hard, was that I had nothing in place to grab on to.

I highly recommend that leaders plan early for their transition—contemplate their relationships and time expenditure—even while they are still working. Think about hobbies, nonprofit interests. Don't wait until you leave your job to think about getting involved in those things—because you just don't know when that end will come.

Now, contrast George's experience with that of another CEO, Sonia. She was informed over a year in advance of her board's transition timeline. With the advance notice, Sonia had time to adjust and plan for the change and commit to transitioning well, so her successor was set up for success. Sonia remembers:

My relationships at work were the hardest thing to leave behind. I had become so close to my team and colleagues over 29 years with the company. It was so hard to walk away from them. However, retirement from my corporate role allowed me to rekindle relationships and emphasize time with my family, which I had largely neglected in my ascension to ever-greater jobs in the company, all of which required extensive international travel.

I was on a public board at the time of my transition, and it was an essential part of transitioning into my Next Season. Board work allowed me to remain involved with the corporate environment in a way that did not compromise family time. Retirement allowed me to take up new hobbies, such as fly fishing and taking trips with friends, which I was never able to do with my work schedule and commitments. I became involved with my college alma mater and now serve them using my skills and experience gained as a corporate executive.

Job One for me in retirement was transitioning my identity and relationships from work to family, friends, and the boards that I opted to join. It required a mental shift on my part, letting go, and grabbing hold of new things.

Another leader of the live-to-work generation described his first day of retirement:

It was the hardest day of my life! The silence from being off email lists, meeting requests, and phone calls was deafening. I could not see beyond my blank calendar and imagined it would remain like this for the rest of my life. I felt sick and tense from head to toe, and began to question who I was and what I would do the rest of my life.

Martha, a Fortune 50 leader, offers this insight:

Many are afraid of retirement because they are losing a long-developed identity. It took me at least a year before I stopped telling people "What I used to do"—almost as though that somehow validated my worth. Establishing your new identity may feel uncomfortable at first, but it is a chance to redefine who you are, what matters most to you, and what you stand for. Take full advantage of it. Embrace the "new you."

And Susie, the spouse of a client, offered her own account of the challenge of breaking free:

Following my husband's retirement, I saw how hard it was for him to shift his paradigm of how the day flows and where to focus. He was addicted to following the stock market, and specifically his former company. He would wake up to see the Wall Street opening bell, watch MarketWatch, and track the performance of his former company throughout the day. He would get depressed if the stock went down and become all knotted up about why, what should be done, etc.—as though he were still in charge. The stock price of his former company literally determined his mood for the day.

Mind you, a chunk of our net worth was tied up with that company's stock, so how it performed was important to us both. But to monitor it compulsively, as he had in his former season? No. It is so important that leaders let go and let themselves break free in order to fully live into their Next Season.

Regardless of the impetus for the transition, even when you choose the timing and conditions, the change can be jarring. Well-intended family and friends ask questions for which you may not have answers (not yet): "What are you going to do now?" "How do you plan to spend your time?" And then come the "Hey, how would you like to . . ." questions, causing even more stress.

The tension of wanting to (still) feel relevant tugs you to think about these invitations, even when they are not exactly what you'd like to do. Secretly living in the dark spaces of your psyche are concerns that these may be the only invites that come your way! More tension, more uncertainty, even when it's because you are so wanted.

Transitioning Does Bring Some Relief

Even if the timing is not of our choosing, most people feel some relief from the transition. Relief from the intensity and business travel. Relief from the dictatorship of your Outlook calendar, from cost-cutting initiatives, from budgets, from justifying spend, from strategic planning sessions, board presentations, earnings calls, performance reviews—everyone experiences some relief, even amid the stress of transitioning.

This is why we tell everyone: First, be kind to yourself. Be patient with yourself (even though most of us are short on patience). Permit yourself to feel down, even slightly depressed, a little lost, and a lot uncertain—feelings that probably are unfamiliar to you, and likely never used to describe you. Your decades-long routines have been abruptly halted, and it is jarring.

Transitioning Also Brings Definite Physical and Psychological Side-Effects

Above all things, be patient with the emotions that run deep, and know that ushering them in the door will also allow you to exit them. Keeping them outside, clamoring to be let in, only delays the confrontation and navigation. This too shall pass— but much like the stages of grief, you have to allow them time and space, in order for you to reach the other side.

What Do Leaders Miss Most Post-Transition?

1. **Company affiliation and relationships.** Leaders miss their colleagues and the comradery. They miss the sense of family and affiliation experienced at work. And they miss feeling the pride of connection to their company/role/people. Many leaders have found their friendships with former colleagues deepened after leaving their company, being no longer encumbered by organizational levels or issues. Several leaders shared stories of former employers intentionally treating re-tirees as "alumni," planfully uniting and engaging with them. Universally, leaders gratefully accept such invitations and the opportunity to stay connected with their previous season in a modest but meaningful way.

2. **Leading people and the satisfaction of watching them succeed.** Those for whom this was impor-

tant seek new roles doing coaching, counseling, and teaching in their Next Season as a way to meaning-fully help others and allow their lessons learned to benefit others.

3. **Being at the heart of complex decisions where their work had impact.** Those who (still) desire to make a difference and have an impact that they can see and measure, are more apt to secure a leadership position in another company or a not-for-profit they care about, or to take a leadership role in a personal endeavor.

Know that You Are Not Alone on This Journey!

MyNextSeason exists because we care about these unavoid-able, critical, and yet fragile career transitions. So please access knowledge like this book—an earlier version of which has helped tens of thousands transition. Connect with others you respect, who have preceded you with a career transition of this magnitude. They, too, will "get it."

Retirement or any challenging transition is a team sport, best not navigated solo. We and others are here for you. We wrote this book for you.

Leanne Caret

Previous Role: President & CEO, Boeing Defense, Space & Security

Retirement Date: December 2022

Next Season Passions:
- Public Board Director
- Blackstone Advisor
- MyNextSeason Advisor

Just Leanne

A few weeks after my retirement, my husband found me crying in our closet. I felt so lost and remember thinking, "What's next? How are we going to do this?" Later, I realized I wasn't afraid of being unhappy. I was anxious because I built my entire identity around my professional position, and now I was just going to be Leanne.

Resounding silence

Figuring out my identity without my corporate title was a huge reinvention. "If I'm not a CEO, who am I?" The thought of no longer getting up at 4:30 a.m. to check email was such a strange concept. Even stranger: when I did go check, there was nothing there. The day immediately after my retirement, there were no emails. Nobody called to ask me questions or get my advice. I thought, "How can I go from being involved in making every critical decision, and in the blink of an eye, I'm no longer even invited to the meeting? Nobody wants my input? How did this happen?"

I had to take some time to figure out what I liked doing and create a plan to build a new sense of self that wasn't rooted exclusively in my career.

Finding clarity

After I retired, I thought I'd have all this wonderful free time to do all the things I wanted. Then I realized I *had* been doing everything I wanted to do. Now I had the daunting task of coming up with a new list.

I was lucky to have the support of MyNextSeason during this time. And I truly feel it saved my life—both emotionally and physically. Working with my Advisor brought such clarity. In times of transition, it is so crucial to have an environment where one can have those darkest, deepest conversations in the sanctity of confidence, with somebody who's incredibly empathetic and helpful. It felt like the greatest medicine of all.

> *I was anxious because I built my entire identity around my professional position, and now I was just going to be Leanne."*

Rooted in purpose

After lots of reflection and work, I realized what I love most is helping people. Now I get to choose who I work with, and I can nurture relationships that bring me joy. I worked to find and create opportunities to collaborate with people I like on issues that align with my priorities. To keep clear sight of those priorities, I drew a tree that showed three branches for areas I wanted to focus on in my Next Season: business relevancy, inspiring future generations, and paying it forward.

I still use my tree to evaluate opportunities and divide my time. And I'm proud to say that I have found activities that fill each branch. I serve on two public boards and as an advisor to a large private equity firm, which keeps my business acumen engaged. I am a MyNextSeason Advisor and work with several universities, which allows me to mentor next-generation leaders. I also work with different groups focused on advancing women—from a policy

perspective to mentoring—paying it forward and passing along insights that have shaped my own journey.

Give grace and grieve

If I could advise someone facing a big transition, it would be this: give yourself grace—your title is gone, your schedule and crazy to-do lists are gone. There's a grieving process that must happen. You're grieving your old life and now you have to start anew.

I felt like a commodity when no one called that very next day! It hurt. But I reminded myself that in any role, our job is to leave it better than we found it, and the next person will do the same. It's not personal—it's the natural progression of a job well done. Finding new purpose and a new everyday cadence is a process, and it's different for everyone. Be kind to yourself.

Choosing the good

If I could be with that Leanne in the early days, who was upset and unsure, I would give her a hug. I would reassure her that her brain won't melt away. She's going to find ways to stay relevant and really help people.

I believe that every morning we make a choice: to have a good day or a bad day. Of course there will be some bad days, but there is so much more opportunity for good if we look for it. Now, when someone asks me for my title, I smile and say, "My name's Leanne."

4

The Pause to Discern

A must-do step in your Next Season journey

You have spent three or four decades advancing your career. Prior to that, you invested years becoming educated, certified, and qualified to practice your profession for as long as you can remember. Since your work is what your life has been mostly about, how can you even imagine what's next?

Discernment Is Crucial, and It Requires a Pause

Here is the main reason why "discernment" is so important: When transitioning, you will experience immense temptation, and pressure, to quickly answer "what will I do next?" But rushing to that answer misses the essential discernment step: listening to your inner voices that have long been hushed. Voices like these:

What do I love to do? What brings me joy? What have I always wanted to spend time on, but was never free to do so? What relationships are important to me? What cracks need to be mended with people I care about? What is my superpower? What do I do/ bring to teams and those with whom I work that is special and uniquely mine? What am I really good at, so that if given the option, I would choose to continue doing again?

This is why discernment is the key entry point in revealing your Next Season. It is being intentional and thoughtful—first, about how you depart your present career, and second, how you explore what you will seek next. Discernment is your first step toward creating a Next Season plan.

For discernment to happen well, you must allow space to be thoughtful, contemplative, reflective, or searching. We call this "the Pause," which allows time/space for deep discernment. This is why we urge our clients to take "the Pause" from the full-on intensity you've been living—before committing to something else.

The Pause requires setting aside time away from the noise and activity of your everyday life and just thinking about yourself, what you enjoy and don't enjoy, and contemplating questions that don't always have easy answers.

If you rush and commit to something too quickly—often something that someone else wants you to do—regret and disappointment may soon follow. Many leaders caught in this trap wish they had taken advantage of The Pause—a detox period to recharge their batteries before summoning the energy to contemplate their next move. Detox priorities are simple but powerful, including sleep, spending overdue time with family/friends, and focusing on personal health and wellness.

While it's ok and healthy to stay busy in the near-term with projects, networking, and exploration during your discernment period, make sure you take the time to be contemplative about the deeper questions and bigger decisions, including what you feel called to do next. Above all else, honor your heart and inner voices.

Here is an example from one of our clients, Mark, who was chief of research for a Fortune 500 company. Mark was excited about retirement and the opportunities to do things he always wanted. However, he confided in his advisor that he was also very nervous. He had so many potential pursuits: join a public company board or two, serve on a non-profit board, write a book, travel, spend more time with family, and be there for his grandchild. The mayor of his town had also asked him to help with several key issues. He feared that retirement would be just as busy as before, now filled with many little things.

But Mark took the opportunity to be thoughtful and discern what he wanted to do next, how he would spend his time. He took The Pause and avoided long-term commitments until he thought it through. He explored opportunities over the next few months, considering what he loved in his work and what he wanted to leave behind, dreaming with his wife, developing a plan. Ultimately, he narrowed it to a portfolio that he loves, including spending Thursday afternoons with his grandchildren.

No Place for Shoulds

Remember in high school, when friends would say, "You're going to college? *Oh, you should go to State!*" "What's your major? *Hey, you should major in Engineering!*" "What do you want to do for the rest of your life? *You should be a doctor, like your dad!*"

So many "shoulds." When you are transitioning, it can feel like that same drill again. Former colleagues, neighbors, relatives, and friends seem to abandon politeness and privacy and share their "expert opinions" on what you *should* do. "You should go on a corporate board." "You should spend time with your children and grandchildren." "You should find a hobby." "You should focus on your health." "You should downsize out of that huge house." "With your experience and gifts, you really should . . ." It seems like everyone has a should to offer, but all that does is add another "s" word to your life: stress.

There is no place for shoulds when it comes to defining how to spend your time. Each person's life looks and feels different, based on personal needs and desires, life goals, constraints (personal, financial, health, geographic), gifts and interests, career experiences, connections/networks, etc. You don't need to accept someone else's view or advice. You are the best expert on you.

Take the case of Kim. Everyone assumed that in retirement, she would pursue something very similar to her long career: financial advising. Kim was the #2 person for one of the largest investment firms in the country.   She was a whiz with numbers, great with people, and a natural leader.

I recall my first conversation with Kim. She shared that she was "done" with anything related to banking/investments—except of course, what was needed for her own retirement—and she was eager to find a way to honor her sister, who became blind when she was 14 years old, and had passed away five years prior to Kim's retirement.

After much discernment on how to best honor her sister, Kim decided to join the board of an organization that trained Seeing Eye Dogs. She brought her big corporate brain and experience to this very fortunate non-profit, helping them triple in size. They halved the cycle time from request to delivery, for placing a Seeing Eye Dog. Kim reports that this effort, requiring only a small fraction of her now-available time, is more rewarding than her storied career as a breaker of many glass ceilings. She found meaningful purpose in her Next Season.

You Have Choices

Throughout your career, you grew accustomed to being decisive and always having a plan, with a ready answer to what's next. That's why it now can be tempting to jump at the first-available opportunity, convincing yourself that it may be the one and only. You might feel that you must have a fully baked plan on Day One. The pressure to make the "right choice" is often embedded with a deeper fear of far-reaching implications that might control your future happiness and fulfillment. That expectation to "choose correctly and quickly" may feel almost paralyzing.

However, the change from corporate life to your Next Season is a real paradigm shift, from a scarcity mentality (no time for anything) to an abundance mentality where "what to do" and "how to spend your time" are limited only by your imagination and physical stamina.

So thankfully, here is the reality: this transition is to your *first* Next Season, not to your *only* next season! Your decision really is: Where to start? Which thing to do first? And rarely are there binding consequences for your initial choice.

Your *first* Next Season is not your *final* one. A bountiful world of options and opportunities await you. So, give yourself permission to take your time as you dream, explore, network, and contemplate future possibilities. You have many Next Seasons to live into!

Your Unique Journey

There are important steps for revealing your Next Season that begin with leaving well (from your former role), transitioning well, and networking with new people who may be helpful/influential/instructional for what you want to do next.

Rarely is this journey a straight line, and it is unique to each person. Discernment can last weeks, months, or longer—and each timeline is ok! Try to avoid the pressure of comparing yourself to others. While some may find their next opportunity more quickly, most clients report it took many conversations, coffees, lunches, and connections first.

No matter what your goals are, seeking guidance from those who have "been there," or who are doing what you are seeking, is invaluable. Your journey is your own, and each step is important!

Doug was incredibly intentional when he worked through the discernment phase, post-retirement. He had many offers on the table, from being a company CEO again, to joining his alma mater's faculty, to boards, to other things from the community. Doug was only 56—so he had a lot of runway ahead. He had been a highly successful and respected public company CEO and Director—and people wanted him.

Doug was sorting through which offers he should spend time evaluating. He and his wife were building a new home, and their three college kids needed some dad-help, so there was no shortage of "stuff" to keep him busy.

To help him sort, we encouraged him to pretend he was waking up in the morning and had to spend a big chunk of the day on "Thing X." Would spending time on it make him want to jump out of bed to work on it, or pull the covers over his head wishing he had said no?

Doug then provided the simplest rephrasing of these questions: "So what you are saying is that if I am not saying 'Hell, yes!' to that idea/opportunity, I need to say 'Hell, no!'" Brilliantly summarized!

Part of the goal in discernment is to ensure you don't recreate the very situation you are trying to escape. Rushing into something often obscures aspects of what will be expected of you, aspects that you'd really not enjoy. For example:

- Leading a non-profit for a cause about which you care deeply may have huge appeal—until you realize the bulk of your time will be spent fund-raising.

- Consulting sounds amazing—you love to advise, help, mentor—until you realize the administrative load of having to sell your services, submit invoices, write proposals, and work with procurement departments to process your contract.

So, take the time to fully understand the details before you commit! You will discover more opportunities over lunches, dinners, on the golf course, at reunions, reading the paper, meeting new people. But you'll need to double-click on these and see which, if any, remain interesting to you.

When you are in your precious few initial detox months, fight the gravitational pull to commit to something significant, time-consuming, longer-term—unless you seek full-time work or need income during that period.

We urge you to take The Pause and consider things from your last job/role/company that you wish to take forward and the parts you prefer to leave behind.

Doug Parker

Previous Role: American Airlines Chairman & CEO

Retirement Date: 2023

Next Season Passions:
- Founder, Breaking Down Barriers
- Corporate Board Director
- CEO Advisor

Look before you leap

As I neared retirement from American Airlines, what would I do next? I loved my career. I felt young and energetic, yet ready for a change. Many voices around me suggested what they thought I should do—but I didn't want to jump into something I might regret. My top three priorities were spending time with my family, focusing on my health, and partnering with my wife, Gwen, to tackle an issue near and dear to both our hearts.

We felt called to action

A deep frustration had bothered me throughout my career: less than 4% of all commercial pilots are persons of color, and only 7% are female. A college degree is not required for a pilot's license, but you *do* need about $100k to attend flight school, and that's a barrier for many. Even worse, you first need to know that this career path *is even available to you*—perhaps the biggest challenge of all.

Right now, we're amid a critical pilot shortage. And we won't get the best-of-the-best if some prospects face barriers to a career they don't even know they can pursue! So Gwen and I decided to take a run at removing these barriers for potential future pilots.

Easier said than done

We started assembling a strategy for scholarships, mentorship, and awareness, but quickly realized we needed help. A friend who funds nonprofits said, "You can't do it yourself. You've got to hire a CEO. You have to get infrastructure in place." So we hired Dana Donati, who was running United Airline's training program. I don't know what we'd do without her! She's an industry expert rather than a nonprofit leader, so she had to learn how 501c3's work, and did so quickly. But what mattered most to us is that she knows the process of becoming a commercial pilot backward and forward.

> **❚❚** *Whenever I explained our nonprofit to people, that's what I started with—Breaking Down Barriers."*

Finding a Name that Said it All

We named our new nonprofit "Breaking Down Barriers." Curious, because there is nothing in that name about pilots or aviation. But whenever I explained our nonprofit to people, that's what I started with—Breaking Down Barriers. "Then that's the right name," Dana said. We can always talk to people about how it's a piloting experience, but what we

want to start with is how we break down the barriers to *becoming* one. There are all these kids out there with enormous potential who don't get to fulfill it because of those barriers.

The power of diverse perspectives

Gwen has always been an amazing thought partner. Through her connections, we found a dynamic group of leaders in the Black community to join our Board. As we met with them, one cautioned us: "Your biggest problem will be: nobody's going to believe you." Why not? "Because a lot of organizations say, 'we're going to send you to college!' and parents are rightly skeptical, because they've been lied to in the past." So we've worked hard to gain credibility, convincing parents and potential students to trust us and our word. Becoming a pro pilot can transform their lives and communities!

Starting small, starting right

We're starting with a dozen eager, smart, dedicated students. Each one is paired with a volunteer professional pilot as a mentor to guide and encourage them, and we already have a backlog of volunteers. Something about our program resonates with them!

We want to scale Breaking Down Barriers the right way, which is the hard part. We must develop concrete plans for expanding and operating more efficiently than at present, with five team members hustling to raise awareness, so we're not in a huge rush.

And we're starting with our own resources on the line: Gwen and I are personally funding the program, along with a generous gift for my retirement from American Airlines. Eventually, we'll need to raise more, but for now we tell folks, "We'll find you when we need you." The blessing is that everyone wants to help, including many pilots interested in mentoring the students. As we learn, we'll grow!

Our students all work other jobs, and then they put in six hours studying each day. The expectation is that, in just a few years, they'll become pilots for major airlines."

The sky's the limit

We now have our first group of students, and I'm amazed. They are so excited! Given my career at American Airlines, I'm a bit embarrassed to admit that I didn't fully appreciate how hard it is to become a pilot! Our students all work other jobs, and then they put in six hours studying each day. The expectation is that, in just a few years, they'll become pilots for major airlines.

Our Next Season of purpose

It's been an incredibly rewarding Next Season for Gwen and myself. I'm also enjoying advising potential CEOs and serving on Quantas Airlines' Board, which has enabled us to explore Australia. I am truly fulfilled helping address an issue critical to our industry and our communities. And this isn't about my legacy—this is about solving a major problem in our industry and our culture. Barriers exist everywhere, and Gwen and I can't fix them all, but we're sure taking a hard run at this one! This is something we can help fix.

For more information about Breaking Down Barriers (BDB), please visit **www.breakingdownbarriers.org**.

5

Prep for Your Earliest Days of Transition

Even before the Pause-to-Discern phase, being prepared for the inevitable barrage of questions and well-meaning advice will save you in those early days

We are often asked: "What comes first?" "What should I be doing now?" "What should I focus on, even as I plan for this transition?"

Through our observations and our clients' feedback, here are five important things that require your attention prior to (or immediately following) a career transition. Be ready with these:

1. Have clear talking points for when you are asked what you are doing next

2. Have a short-term project to focus on (while you develop a longer-term plan)

3. Have someone to talk to—honestly, vulnerably (as you think through what's next)

4. Seek alignment with your spouse/partner (on priorities for you together, and individually)

5. Have your "self-marketing materials" ready (like LinkedIn and a bio, in case something interesting your way comes)

Let's take a deep look at each of these prep points, including examples we know you'll relate to.

1. Have clear talking points for what you are doing next

The questions will begin as soon as the news is out: "What are you going to do next?" This is why you need to be prepared! You may feel both anticipatory stress and in-the-moment stress about how to respond—if you have not formulated a clear answer yet. And if you hesitate to answer (or even if you don't hesitate), your audience will leap to offer well-intended advice about what you *should* do next (here's that dreaded *should* again).

Our best advice:

- Have your talking points ready (rehearsed, and in your head) to share what you'll be doing next . . .
- . . . and be sure to include two magic words: *for now*

Having prepared responses in your head, ready to share, has two main benefits: it will be calming for you to be prepared, and in most cases, it will deter the asker from probing for more, enabling you to steer the conversation elsewhere. We also urge our clients to always include the words *"for now,"* so it leaves open the notion that this "plan" may change (because it will, as we all know).

Here are some actual talking points our clients have used:

....

- *"I am exploring some advisor options with a couple of companies who have reached out. **For now,** I want to enjoy time at home, reconnect with my family. After 32 years of a career I loved, I am in no hurry to jump to what's next!"*

- *"I'm active in conversations with a few former co-workers about a range of things . . . **For now,** I am excited to play a* *little more golf, spend more time with the grandkids, and do some traveling with my spouse."*

- ***"For now,** I am excited to get back in shape, reconnect with my husband, and improve my golf game."*

- *"I am enjoying thinking about possibilities. I will continue my board work as I explore other possibilities. **For now,** I am just happy to have a little more freedom and time—and I am nowhere near ready to give that up."*

- *"I am exploring possible board work and some private equity projects my buddies are involved in. **For now,** I am enjoying not having to hop on an airplane for business—and being free to see friends and family."*

- ***"For now,** I'm thinking about a range of things—and know that whatever I decide on, it will allow me to spend more time with my family, work on my health, and not miss any of my grandson's Little League games."*

- *"I've still got a lot of gas in my tank—so **for now,** am actively exploring different possibilities that won't require me to relocate. I'll be happy to share with you, once I've landed."*

An obvious benefit of having a ready response is so the person will stop inquiring, unless it's something you want to talk with them about. It's not that you don't want to share, or that you are being dismissive, dishonest, or disrespectful. It's simply that you probably don't have it figured out yet—which is understandable at this point. It can also be frustrating to get into all that with everyone over and over again!

In most cases, people's questions are well-meaning, from those who care about you, admire you, and want only the best for you. However, it doesn't diminish your stress of not having a clear, confident answer to how you are going to spend your Next Season!

Having a clear response will quiet the noise you wish to quiet, and usher in an alternate conversation you welcome more readily.

2. Have a short-term project to focus on while you develop a longer-term plan

We've already discussed the importance of having space for contemplation, reflection, conversations with others, and exploration of what else is going on around you. This is *The Pause for Discernment.*

We typically recommend a Pause of about 3 to 12 months, depending on your situation, including your personal health (physical and mental), how clearly you feel called to what you will do next, and what else is buzzing in your life. Some people need more time, some less.

But pressing Pause doesn't mean full stop. We find that clients do best when they still have goals to focus on. Use this time to sample things in which you may have long-term interest, like teaching a class for a semester, or living a few months in a new location you are considering. Tackle things you've wanted to, but haven't had the time, like reconnecting with family or friends, setting up your home office, traveling more, or finally organizing those thousands of family photos.

"Permeability" in whatever project you choose is important. Pick a project that has great interest and personal value to you, but one that also leaves you time to explore other options. We have heard this over and over from our clients: it helps to have an immediate project, but not to be so booked that you can't explore longer-term possibilities.

Here's a fine example of a short-term project from Joan, CFO of a global company:

On a girl's trip for my 55th birthday, I shared with my daughters that, one day, I wanted to learn how to quilt like my grandmother. So, for Christmas, they bought me a top-of-the-line sewing machine to realize my dream! This happened two years before

I retired, so the machine sat in its box, collecting dust, while I continued to work.

My company was navigating a lot of change, so my last two years on the job were a blur. I had never worked such long days in my 38-year corporate career! As I prepared to "retire" from the company, I couldn't shake the visual of that unopened box and all it represented about the past two years.

So, as I began to think through what I wanted to do in my Next Season, I quickly landed on an immediate priority: to get sewing lessons near our beach house where I planned to spend my first summer following my transition. And that's just what I did. During those next few months, when I was learning how to make quilts with my new machine, I also looked longer-term, talking with people who were still recruiting me for boards, college adjunct positions, and local non-profits.

By Fall, exactly 7 months after my last day at work, I decided to begin teaching a finance class at a local college, and to join the board of a private equity company focused on a space of long interest to me.

Sewing was my shorter-term project to focus on while I made longer-term plans. And my quilt-making continues even as I have added new professional activities to my Next Season portfolio.

While it may be exciting to tackle those "to-dos" that have been waiting, make sure you keep space in your calendar to be spontaneous and put both yourself and your family first. As our client John found out, that time can quickly become precious.

I was CEO of a Financial Services company in my last role. But my successful career ended earlier than expected, because my carefully groomed successor was ready, and the company didn't want to risk my successor being recruited by a competitor because the top job wasn't yet available. So my transition came earlier than anticipated.

My job required global travel, countless hours away on business trips, and many missed family events. I worked hard to stay in touch with extended family members, but I was often just the check-writer, since I never could take time away from work to participate in more meaningful ways.

Shortly after my exit, while discerning what to do next, my sister called from halfway across the country: she was diagnosed with terminal cancer. So I immediately took up residence with her in Arizona, as her primary support person. I drove her to appointments, helped manage her home affairs, ensured she took her meds and ate healthy meals. Three months later, she passed away.

This was one of the hardest, yet most rewarding periods of my life. I felt honored to be her primary caregiver when she needed support the most, and I was so grateful to have had the time to be physically present and helpful to her. I could not have done this, had I not transitioned ahead of plan. Thus, I found myself newly grateful for what had initially been an unwelcomed timing of my transition to retirement.

3. Have someone to talk to—honestly and vulnerably—as you think through what's next

Discovering your Next Season is never a straight line. You consider possible paths, sample them when possible, talk with people on those paths, evaluate, and continue on your current path—or modify it and try again. Each cycle creates its own progress and momentum toward finding your Next Season.

This continual rethinking, trial-&-error, is best done in live conversation with a "thought partner," someone you deeply trust, with whom you can bare your soul. Through conversation and contemplation, you'll continually revisit your thinking and retest your ideas. Here's an example from one of our Advisors, who was working with Bill:

When Bill and I first met, he was fairly certain he knew what he wanted to do: get on a couple of boards. Bill had been CEO of two global business units during his 42-year career and had a lot of exposure to his company's board. He loved business, solving problems, and people. So, board work sounded like the perfect role for him.

But as we worked through the discernment process, I asked him questions. *What do you enjoy doing? If you could erase one activity from your calendar, never to do again, what would it be? What are your priorities for this next phase?* And so on.

Bill's answers: *Well, I hate meetings . . . I'd love not to have to sit through long meetings anymore. And I'd like control of my calendar. My wife and I are building a home on the Islands and I want to go there when we like—and not live by my Outlook calendar telling me when I can or can't take off.*

I like solving problems—and I get frustrated, as an engineer by training, when I have to just sit there and wait for others to figure it out . . . I'd prefer to jump in and fix it.

I echoed what I heard back to him, as if I were a video camera capturing his testimony. Being the brilliant person he is, I didn't need to say more. He quickly reached the same conclusion I had: all the things that are important to him—that he wants to do—or not do—are *utterly incompatible with a public company Directorship!*

So he revisited what mattered to him in this Next Season, and moved forward with a new plan: he decided to be certified as an arbitrator, and an advisor to other corporate leaders who aspired for seniormost roles.

Had Bill not had someone to engage with and reflect back honestly what they heard him say, he might have continued down a path that would have been disappointing at best.

Everyone needs a thought partner to iterate ideas with—someone who knows you, cares about you, and is willing to be honest with you. It can be a close colleague or friend, a sibling with whom you are close, or a professional coach/advisor. Working through "what's next" is not a solo sport! Be sure you have someone you trust, with whom you can be vulnerable, to work this process.

4. Seek alignment with your spouse/partner on priorities for you together, and individually

We cannot overstate how important this is! The person who will be most impacted by your career change, other than yourself, is your spouse or partner. They have been up-close on this journey with you for a long, long time . . . and have had to make their own adjustments, accommodations, and concessions in some cases, to enable your success. Whether this person worked outside your home or not, they have been powerfully impacted by your career, so any big change like retirement obviously impacts them as well.

This transition time presents a wonderful opportunity for you two to align on what is most important to you both, what you hope to accomplish in this Next Season, individually and together. What are each of your visions for what, and how much, you will do together? And what do each of you hope to do independent of one another?

Check out Frank's story:

As I planned my retirement, I spent time with my wife Kathleen, talking about initial thoughts of what I wanted to do, what she wanted to do, what we wanted to do together, and how we could help each other.

This dialog was incredibly helpful. But my biggest a-ha was discovering Kathleen's biggest fear: that I would end up as busy as I had been in my job! She reminded me of many family vacations interrupted when I had to leave for board meetings or crises. She did not want that in our Next Season! I agreed of course, and put boundaries in place to ensure that wouldn't happen. Our initial conversation became ongoing as we continued to work on understanding and supporting each other's dreams.

There are many different approaches you and your spouse/partner can take as you discuss and agree to your priorities in this Next Season. The important part is (1) set aside time for this, and (2) discuss with intentionality, honestly and openly, your respective priorities, so you can support each other in what you wish to do together, and what you wish to do in your healthy independence.

Of course, there are some common pitfalls in doing this! Our clients shared these:

- *Thinking you will share a home office.* Well, maybe. Can you work effectively beside one another? Or does each of you need quiet space or privacy? Shared offices are often a romantic notion with an unsatisfying ending.

- *Not clarifying how chores will be shared.* Who will prepare meals, do the grocery shopping, walk the dog, etc.? (A famous quote: "I married you for better and for worse . . . but not for lunch!")

- *Missing the chance to fully understand/support each other's priorities and agenda.* Are you focusing too much on your own issues/priorities?

- *Missing out on shared activities together due to not communicating.* What activities can you do together, like working out, walking the dog, or enjoying a quick get-away?

These pitfalls can be avoided by getting aligned with your spouse/partner on shared and individual priorities—so you can support one another.

5. Have your professional materials ready in case something interesting your way comes

It is so important that your story is well told—and there is no better person to tell it than you. It'll always be fun to share highlight reels and war stories from your career, but remember —who you are is far more than your old roles. Your challenge now is to reframe your experience and accomplishments in a way that clearly articulates *the impact you will have on new interests.*

This is the time to talk about who you *want to be*—rather than *who you were*. This isn't always easy, and many leaders tell us it can be downright uncomfortable.

Taking time to discern and think deeply about what's next informs your new story, and increases your confidence in networking. It may come in the form of written materials like a resume, or it may simply be creating a strong personal value proposition or new elevator pitch that succinctly states the value you bring as you have conversations.

If your professional materials are out-of-date, we recommend refreshing them to reflect your current interest, or your early thinking about where you might land. Consider updating the following:

- A complete bio
- Your resume
- Your LinkedIn profile
- If applicable, a short speaker bio and list of speaking events and publications

Each of these speaks to who you are, your work history, and what you are focused on now. You are no longer your former title, but rather a leader who brings a lifetime of experience and expertise to a new passion.

In updating your materials, you may find the process to be just as important as the product. Walking through your career history helps you look back on your experience through a new lens and rediscover important themes about yourself, both professionally and personally. It also offers the opportunity to practice speaking about your experience and telling your story in a new way. This gives you ready-made talking points for networking and interviews.

Ultimately, your materials should tee you up for great conversations as you transition. With your new story in hand, you can confidently launch your new personal brand into the market—on paper, in person, and online.

Peter Lichtenthal

Previous Role: Global Brand President, The Estée Lauder Companies

Retirement Date: 2017

Next Season Passions:
- Business Leadership Consultant
- Not-for-profit Board Director
- Guest Lecturer, Brandeis University
- MyNextSeason Advisor

You are now your own enterprise

Executives are powerful leaders. We develop and execute strategies. We have assistants. We have people awaiting our decisions. Letting go of these trappings can be challenging! When I retired, I realized that I was trading that power for full control of my life. At first, all that control seemed scary, because I realized I was responsible for every decision I was making. It was both a burden and a blessing—because it was on me to decide. As I explain it to others: you are now your own enterprise. You are now managing your life and career the way you managed your business unit before. With that comes: What is my business plan? Where are my information gaps? How do I tap into my network to reach my goals?

Titles are temporary . . . brands are timeless

Letting go of a title like Global Brand President, I wondered: How I would be perceived? How would I remain relevant and productive? I learned that I didn't need the title for people to perceive me as a strong leader. I brought my personal brand with me. I'm just focusing it differently and in a way that taps into my interests and priorities in my Next Season.

Filtering the noise

People wondered how I would translate or evolve my leadership, title, and style into a much different way of working. Sometimes I had to filter the noise of "What are you going to do with your time?" That's well-intended, but not always helpful. I learned to stick to my guns on why I made my decision. I listened to the best they offered and filtered reactions not relevant to me.

Stay true to who you are

My current activities all involve education or mentorship. I started my own leadership development LLC. I advise a wide range of clients for MyNextSeason. I'm an adjunct professor at my alma mater. And I'm chair of a not-for-profit that supports LGBTQ students with scholarships and leadership training. I've always had a passion for mentoring, but it's different when not under a corporate umbrella. It's more personal, and I find that extremely rewarding.

Balance isn't always easy

I chose to retire at 61, and I looked forward to it. The result has been even more positive than I thought! I now appreciate how many interests I can incorporate into my days. However, it takes ongoing vigilance to keep my priorities straight and make sure I'm not pursuing more than I want to take on. That means being able to course-correct—expand my time with some activities and pull back on others. But the interesting thing has been the learning curve of being the one who decides. I have to be disciplined: "How do I want to enjoy my time, and what's going to give me the best balance?"

> **"**
> *I learned that I didn't need the title for people to perceive me as a strong leader. I brought my personal brand with me."*

Pivoting from uncertainty to confidence

When you retire and new opportunities haven't kicked in yet, it can be a difficult time, because you're acutely aware of what you're leaving behind. I was open to help with this transition, and the MyNextSeason process gave me  armor and confidence to move forward that I didn't think I needed, but in actuality I did. It's what I now try to give to others as an Advisor. When I work with clients on what is important to them, what they can start researching and investigating and adding to their life now, the excitement level starts really growing and letting go becomes easier.

A big perk of letting go

The ability to go on vacation free of anxiety, emails, and texts is amazing. I used to wonder what's going on, what email am I missing? Now I say, wow, what a difference for my mind to be completely free. That joy has never stopped!

Looking toward the future ...

I look forward to exploring a corporate board seat and expanding the variety of my executive advising and mentoring. Over the past few years, my clients have become increasingly diverse in life stage and career. That keeps me sharp, exposing me to different people's needs. I grow from that.

... While honoring the past

If you had a gratifying career, how could you not miss certain things? But that is supplanted by a whole new world of opportunity and excitement. It's normal and a nice thing, like smiling at something, looking back in fondness.

6

The Importance of Health

When you transition from a big job into your Next Season, focusing on your health is actually job #1.

Many leaders put their health on hold as they travel the world, crisscrossing time zones at the speed of business. For growing companies, "crazy-busy quarters" turn into "crazy-busy years," and with success comes increased demand and pressure.

It is not unusual for high-performing leaders to take meds for high blood pressure or cholesterol, or prescription sleep aids to quiet their minds after stressful days. Exercise time gets squeezed out by early morning flights, late meetings, late dinners. Business dinners always include alcohol and seldom feature greens or grains. And so your personal health can suffer as you give the company your best.

Living fully into your Next Season means having the physical health to do so! Now is the time to spotlight this more than you may have done in the past. MyNextSeason's Medical Concierge, Dr. Jennifer Daley, offers this prescription for your health:

As a leader, you've spent sleepless nights mentally preparing, planning, or worrying about big meetings, big decisions, and big initiatives. It might seem that transitioning out of this world would reduce stress, but transferring these responsibilities and being unsure of "what's next" may still have you tossing and turning. Transitions, whether welcomed and well-thought-out or not, bring about stress—a natural response to this significant change and a busy life. Now is the perfect time to reset!

Your dynamic career may have submerged exercise and nutrition under your priority list. So, in my role as one of MyNextSeason's Medical Concierges, I meet one-on-one with clients to discuss family history, caretaking responsibilities, health and wellness concerns, and goals. Below are some suggestions for creating a solid foundation for both nutrition and stress management.

Really Eating Healthy

What does it mean to "eat healthy" today? Bookstore shelves are filled with countless approaches: low-fat, Keto, clean eating, juicing, vegan, etc. With so much confusion surrounding this question, here are my seven easy-to-follow recommendations for healthy eating:

1. Eat a minimum of 100 grams (roughly 3.5 ounces) of healthy proteins each day, like Greek yogurt, oatmeal, lean meats, fish, beans, and non-fat cheese. Functional medicine health advisors recommend consuming 30+ servings of plants each week. (Note: Read food labels carefully, noting grams of protein, carbohydrates, and fat. Avoid foods that have a high proportion of carbohydrates-to-protein or high levels of saturated fat.)
2. Eat an unlimited amount of green leafy vegetables— adding fruit in moderation.
3. Avoid eating white carbohydrates (like bread, rice, potatoes, pasta, processed foods).
4. Eat a moderate amount of non-saturated fats (like olive oil, safflower oil, canola oil, nuts, and nut butters).
5. Drink eight 8-ounce glasses of water each day (that totals 2 quarts).

6. Stop eating 2 hours before bedtime.
7. See your doctor before starting any diet to ensure you are in good health.

Really Managing Stress

You may know some methods to reduce stress. But putting them into action during a time of storm or flux is challenging! Instead of reaching for that glass of wine, cookie, or iPad, try these solid, time-tested techniques to restore a sense of calm and presence. Your ultimate goal: increasing the enjoyment of your life!

- Get outside and into nature
- Enjoy music (either listening or performing)
- Exercise
- Eat healthy, nutritious foods
- Relax into healthy sleep patterns
- Read or write poetry
- Spend time with animals—maybe it's the right time for a pet
- Connect with friends and family—nurture your relationships
- Laugh
- Light a scented candle
- Take up gentle yoga practice
- Meditate
- Join social groups through church, volunteering, hobbies, and sports

Whatever you choose to do next, health and wellness will be your biggest and most essential asset.

Taking Stock of Your Health and Wellbeing

One thing our medical team urges is self-assessment—taking stock of where you may need to focus to realign your health in your Next Season. A simple tool like the one below can be a helpful start in thinking through where you may need to get additional help on your journey to being your best physical self.

Health & Wellness Self-Assessment

CATEGORIES	🙂	😐	🙁	ACTION
Physical Health/Wellbeing				
Sleep				
Stamina/Energy level				
Sense of Purpose/Optimism				
Activity Level – Cardio				
Activity Level – Strength				
Movement – Balance & Flexibility				
Up to date physicals				
Stress Management				
Relationship Health				
Joy, Happiness, Hopefulness				
Engagement in Nonwork Interests				

So often, our lack of attention to health/wellbeing is rooted in our unwavering dedication to work. We miss routine exercise, routine health checks/scans, and other steps that help prevent health problems and illness. It's crazy how months turn into years when it comes to when you had your last checkup, last mammogram, last colonoscopy!

And if work demands weren't enough, so many in our age bracket are navigating other demanding life streams: supporting kids in higher education and caring for others, including children, aging parents, other family, or neighbors in need. It's a lot—and it takes its toll.

You cannot help others unless you are at your best. Recommit to your personal health and wellbeing. Visit your local gym or hire a trainer to help you customize a program for your age and any health restrictions. While humbling to acknowledge, it's necessary to remember that you probably can't resume the activities you did in your 20's, with the same degree of intensity. Movement is so important! We need to challenge ourselves while being cautious so we don't incur injuries due to lack of proper conditioning or overzealous actions.

One of our clients, Jim, tells this story:

I was so on top of my health for most of my career! A life-long runner, I was disciplined in eating and exercise and keenly aware of how important my runs were to coping with job stress and mental health.

But then, with great shock and sadness, my college freshman son started using drugs and got into legal trouble. My non-work (and often at-work) time and attention turned entirely to my son and his mounting issues—and almost simultaneously, I stopped running. I started eating poorly and drinking too much alcohol to soothe the stress and cope with the unthinkable.

These life events and my own malaise triggered a premature retirement—not with joy in my heart, but out of a sheer need for time and relief from job expectations I could no longer fulfill . . . and so I could focus on helping my son.

Gary Scheffer, former head of Global Communications at GE, shares his own experience:

My decision to retire was, in large part, because I wanted to improve my health. My company offered excellent health and fitness programs and encouraged their use, but the long hours at my desk and global travel really took their toll. I put on weight and wasn't sleeping enough. It was no one's fault but my own— the long hours and lack of exercise were my choice. I needed to change the dynamic.

Since deciding to retire a year ago, I've lost 30 pounds. At the risk of sounding like a TV infomercial, I am surprised at how easy it's been. First, the consultation with MyNextSeason's medical concierge, Dr. Jennifer Daley, opened my eyes to how bad my diet was. Her suggestion to switch to a low-carb, high-protein diet really got me started. Second, I had more time to return to a reasonable exercise routine. I love running and biking, and combined with my new diet, the weight came off quickly.

This summer I am spending a week with a former profession-al cyclist, riding the Blue Ridge Mountains of South Carolina. I never had time to do this in my old job, nor the time to train for it. I'd love to do more of these physical travel adventures in the next few years, but first I am going to see if I successfully make it up and down South Carolina's peaks!

One of my goals is to continue being physically active for as many years as possible. So, I'll need to add something like yoga classes to maintain my flexibility and strength. I have also done a little work with a personal trainer, who pushes me harder than I would myself. It's been very helpful.

I consider myself very lucky to have the support of my wife, who is a great athlete herself—a strong swimmer and cyclist. She encourages me and is a big help with my new diet. She booked the South Carolina trip for me as a Christmas gift and also goes with me on cycling charity rides.

My biggest obstacle going forward is likely to be my old hab-its—the enduring lure of a pepperoni pizza or a steak sandwich. But I have to say, a lack of time to exercise was always my main challenge. As I consider new roles, I want to make sure that I have time to maintain my health.

Staying motivated has never been a problem, because I re-ally enjoy exercising. I have learned, however, that if I channel my competitiveness into a bike ride with friends or a road race, it really helps. So I sign up for a lot of things and focus on doing my best. Yes, I am "that guy" at your local 5K road race who is way too intense!

My advice to other transitioning leaders: apply some of your old corporate discipline and focus on health and fitness goals that you can measure against yourself—whether losing weight or train-ing for an event. Improving your health will make your Next Sea-son not only longer, but much more enjoyable!

Healing Isn't Just Physical

Another form of healing comes from accepting the terms under which you transition. If you are happy with the terms, there is no problem.

But if the transition is not of your choosing, you have a speed bump to navigate. The emotional side-effects are very real, and a new set of burdens is immediately upon you: What do I tell my family? What do I say to former colleagues and direct reports—especially if I disagreed with the decision, the choice of my successor, or the organization's direction? What do I tell friends?

This is a "traumatic transition" of the corporate variety— and the toll, physically and emotionally, is real. Yet, you must move forward, one foot in front of the other. You can do this!

But it takes a little time . . . and it starts with something you might not think of: *forgiving yourself.* You are not to blame for the change; it is not of your making. And the circumstances of your departure are not your colleagues' focus. They are centered on your impact while you were there, and their sadness at your leaving.

Allow people to celebrate you, thank you, appreciate you for what you did for them. That is heartfelt and sincere. Allow those kind words to be part of your healing balm. Those impacts are part of your legacy and the gifts you leave behind.

There *will* be a Next Season for you—and that's what we're here to help you discover.

The Good Fortune of This Time

We are so fortunate to live in a time when there is new information daily about longevity and the role and importance of nutrition, movement, sleep, hydration, and relationships. Pioneers like Mark Hyman, MD have been educating us about Functional Medicine and its importance for decades. *Younger Next Year* by Chris Crowley and Henry Lodge, MD, was first published in 2004. A breakthrough in its time, and updated several times since, the book draws on the latest science of aging, teaching how to become functionally younger each year, and even offers customized counsel for women versus men. Peter Attia, MD's *Outlive: The Science and Art of Longevity* continues to top the best-seller list, providing an easy-to-understand guide that draws on the latest knowledge of science and the body, for a healthier whole you: optimizing sleep, nutrition, exercise, and emotional health. And that's just scratching the surface of what's out there.

We can go a long way toward educating ourselves, solidifying the practices that are serving us well, engaging in new behaviors—with the help of others, whether it be our primary care docs, health coaches, exercise trainers, etc. There is nothing more important for us to do than ensure we care for ourselves.

With transitions of any kind comes stress. Your mind and body are enduring intense changes. So, be kind to your body. Honor it. Limit alcohol intake. Get outside to regain perspective on the world around you. Time spent outside in nature helps so much.

Learning From Our Youngers

We are seeing in the next generation a deeper understanding and respect for the Whole You—and for work-life balance. We can learn so much from their intentionality and honoring of their bodies and life balance. One of our clients, Connie, shared her practice of "reverse mentoring" where she pulled together a group of younger advisors—to listen to them, how they do things, and learnings they had. They provide not only inspiration, but wisdom and clarity that brings great value to our understanding of things.

Another client, Valerie, shared this story:

. . . .

My primary care doctor was adamant that I increase my protein intake as part of my weight-loss strategy. It was my 29-year old son who recommended drinking a powdered protein drink in the morning after exercising—and my 26-year old daughter who sent me a recipe for a quinoa-vegetable-protein salad that she makes every Sunday and brings to work in her bento box along with crunchy vegetable sticks each day. Both of them are slender, strong, and work out regularly—and offered me advice I had not thought of. I now check in regularly with each of them, and listen to their friends as they speak—to learn new practices for healthier living.

. . . .

Geri Thomas

Previous Role: Chief Diversity Officer & Georgia State President, Bank of America

Retirement Date: 2016

Next Season Passions:
- Founder, GPT Consultants
- Advisory & NFP Board Member
- MyNextSeason Advisor

Clean break

When I retired from Bank of America after 45 years, I was purposeful in leaving behind my role and stepping into my next chapter. When people came to me looking for professional or industry advice, I was more than happy to connect them with other people still working in the space, but I was intentional about shifting my energy to a new focus.

I wanted to start engaging with the world as myself, not as "The Bank." For me, it was a bit easier since I am an Atlanta native and have always been involved in a lot of community work that was not professionally driven.

A balance of Next Season pursuits

Today, I have a broad portfolio of interests. I started my own consulting LLC, and I am an advisor at MyNextSeason. I also serve on the advisory board for the business school at Georgia State and on the board of redefinED atlanta, a nonprofit working to drive systemic improvement in K-12 public education. It is a very rewarding combination of activities that also allows me the freedom to pursue my passion for travel and exploring new cultures—which is a top priority.

Making health a priority

I recognized early on that to live the vibrant life I envisioned for myself post-retirement, I had to be healthy. So, eight years ago, I started going to a trainer, and I still go to that trainer today. Everybody knows it. I don't miss it.

I do it because I want stamina. I want strength and flexibility. I want to be able to go and do and not be held back by any physical limitations. Who knows what my productivity would have been if I had started focusing on my physical health earlier, but I can tell you, at 73 years old, it really makes my life work for me now. My days are so full; it's amazing to think that I ever had time to work before!

> **"**
> *I recognized early on that to live the vibrant life I envisioned for myself post-retirement, I had to be healthy."*

Real results

If I hadn't committed to my training, I wouldn't be able to do the things that I'm enjoying so much today. I just came back from an amazing trip to Spain, where it was 102 degrees, and we walked about four miles a day. It was horribly hot, but thankfully, I wasn't too physically taxed and was up for the adventures of each new day.

Setting boundaries for mental health

Mental well-being is just as important as physical health. I think another essential practice I have started in my next chapter is setting boundaries.

When you're working for someone else, it's hard to set boundaries about what you want to or are willing to do. Being able to say no and not feeling bad about it has been so important in this phase of my life.

It was kind of hard for me to put those boundaries in place initially. But now I have no hesitation and no guilt. People have come to just know: No, I'm not taking on that type of work. I'm not able to have a call today. I don't do breakfast meetings. I'm not going to start before 9 am.

Stress of transition

I've noticed the stress that retirement transition can have on colleagues and clients. I think it is key to recalibrate how you view your value and what is most important to you. In my coaching, I try to help clients realize that it's ok to experience a sense of loss as their routines change but to remember who they are and what they know will not be lost.

I enjoy supporting people as they identify what they want and explore how they can achieve it, reminding them they have the power to make life decisions that are in their best interest and in the direction that they will find happiness.

Measure by joy

While I attribute part of my ability to live a fulfilling life since retirement to focusing on physical and mental fitness—it also really comes down to choosing joy. In my opinion, there is really nothing that you HAVE to do in life. If something doesn't make you happy—an activity or relationship is not bringing you joy—don't do it.

7

The Importance of Relationships

They will nurture you and lengthen your life

By the close of your career, it's not unusual to have strain in your relationships with your life partner or family—or to feel you have few real friends outside of work. After years of missing events, taking calls, working during family vacations, and living in a world of "confidential," it can be hard to maintain close ties with others.

It's no wonder many find themselves feeling alone and stressed, just when they most need friends, and most need a support system to bridge from old to new. Socializing, which was so much fun and energizing at the beginning of your career, often becomes stressful and exhausting by the end. Thus, at a time when you most need friendships and companionship to help process your transition, these may be a scarce commodity.

The Health Impact of Relationships

The research is very clear: relationships directly correlate to longevity. People who have meaningful friendships are physically healthier and live longer. Quoting WebMD Chief Medical Officer Dr. John Whyte: "With lower rates of heart disease, cognitive decline, obesity, and other common ailments, social people enjoy longer lives. For those who suffer from any type of disease, loneliness has been shown to reduce lifespan." Loneliness also is associated with greater sensitivity to pain, immune system suppression, diminished brain function, and lower quality and quantity of sleep.

The longest longitudinal study by Harvard University (85 years and counting) has tracked what keeps people healthy and happy. Persistently and consistently, one factor stands out, tying physical health, to mental health, to longevity: good relationships. Warm relationships. Caring relationships. Drs. Waldinger and Schultz, who direct the Harvard Study, summarize it well:

"Over and over again, when the participants in the Harvard Study reached their 70s and 80s, they would make a point of saying that what they valued most were their relationships with friends and family. If we accept the wisdom—and, more recently, the scientific evidence—that our relationships are among our most valuable tools for sustaining health and happiness, then choosing to invest time and energy in them today becomes vitally important. It is an investment that will affect everything about how we live in the future."

Here is some wisdom from co-author and MyNextSeason co-founder Mark:

The Power of Relationships Changed My Life

In mid-2012, I reflected on the prior five years. At the time, I was Treasurer of Bank of America and thought back on the financial crisis: the summer and fall of 2008, the Lehman and Merrill weekend, the bank downgrades, the capital raises. Our family had moved twice—from London to New York, and then to Charlotte. My daughters' school schedules forced me to commute for seven months with each move. My days were long and adrenaline-filled, and my nights often sleepless as I mentally prepared for the next day or worried about the next crisis.

While taking stock of my life and events of prior years, I asked my wife Becky some questions. (Full disclosure: I was apprehensive about what I might hear!) I asked her: *How have I been doing as a husband and father? Am I spending enough time with you and our three girls? Am I around enough?*

I never expected what Becky said. She was concerned that I seemed to focus entirely on work and our family, but nothing external. I'd abandoned time with our friends and extended family, she said. Seeing my work permeate my mind and mood, she felt strongly that I needed something else to engage my heart, mind, and time.

That conversation was a gift-wrapped wake-up call! I was unable to shake her words as I prepared to retire from Bank of America and co-found MyNextSeason. Becky was right, but how could I fit more into my schedule?

I always valued relationships, but in truth, I had taken no time in the preceding five years to build new ones or maintain old ones. This had to change!

I started prioritizing time to deepen relationships with several friends and establish new ones. This required my being intentional about scheduling friends for an early breakfast, a coffee, or an evening drink. I had to make the time to spend time with people I cared about.

Shortly after my conversation with Becky, I reconnected with a friend who invited me to a golfing weekend. My gut reaction was swift: I did not have the time for golfing with friends! Our girls' schedules dictated things I needed to attend. My home to-do list was long. And frankly, I was a horrible golfer.

Thankfully, I consulted my best personal advisor (Becky). She strongly encouraged my going—and after much agonizing, I said yes. I realized it was an opportunity to strengthen several important relationships and possibly build new ones.

The weekend was a blast! The relationships I formed that weekend are among my closest today. As a bonus, I realized that the challenging, invigorating sport of golf clears my mind as it helps me build relationships. (And I have improved, by the way!)

As I considered retiring, those friends helped me think through what I needed to add back into my life and dream about my future again. In addition to occasional rounds of golf, I joined two not-for-profit boards and began mentoring a group of young business professionals on business and faith.

It has been ten years since I retired from my banking career, and I am so grateful to those friends who cared enough to help me through the transition and encourage me to pursue passions outside of work. My friends helped me think about finishing my job well and processing my own Next Season. And they continued to be there for me, to brainstorm and bounce ideas as we started MyNextSeason and began to grow it.

We've shared ideas, advice, challenges . . . not to mention lots of great food . . . and none of that would have happened, had I not paused to take stock of my life, and been open to observations and coaching from friends who knew me well and loved me, and been open to reordering my life's priorities.

I still remember the feeling in my stomach as I asked those questions of Becky. I never realized her answer and encouragement would have such a profound impact on my future.

By the time you honor your work commitments, family obligations, and time with work-friends, which is often needed to keep things "healthy" at work, there is little to no time to focus on friendships outside of work.

The sad reality is that when the transition from work happens, often those "work friends" disappear . . . especially if they are still working. It can be an incredibly lonely time—and a reminder of the importance of focusing effort in this space and growing new friendships.

Here is a cautionary tale from our client Charlie:

....

I was a superstar, admired at my company, revered in my field, a valued leader. When I retired, universities recruited me as a teacher, strategic advisor, executive-in-residence. I began writing a book.

Before my planned retirement, I bought a dream boat for sharing the Florida seascape with my children and grandchildren, fishing, exploring, and enjoying life together.

Unexpectedly, my 37-year executive career was terminated by my CEO, whom I had supported for a decade! My CEO was laser focused on getting my successor firmly in place before he stepped down. And so, to my utter shock and dismay, I endured an "accelerated transition out." I was devastated and embarrassed, questioning all I had believed about my tenure, impact, and worth.

Adding to my angst was this crushing irony: as a leader, I had ushered many others into "accelerated retirement," ahead of their plans and desires—because "it was the right thing for the business." But when I was fast-tracked out the door, I never imagined it could be so hard.

I spoke by phone with my MyNextSeason Advisor. We were supposed to discuss my pursuits in my Next Season, but I was nowhere near ready to talk about that! I was at the marina with my boat, alone. I'd asked my wife to join me for a day of boating, but she had committed to take our granddaughter shopping. So I had no one else to invite.

I was hurting, consumed by recognizing that I was alone, watching others head off to fish and boat with friends.

I realized that I had no real friends. No one to invite boating or even to lunch. No one would understand my injured heart and weakened self-confidence.

Earlier in my career, my wife and I had become close friends with another work couple. The husband worked for me, and our wives quickly became best friends. But everything went awry when the company went through a down-sizing and I had to let my friend go. It took years for my wife to recover from the hurt and loss of that friendship and we vowed never to mix work with friends again. The challenge is when work consumes all of your time, there is little to nothing left for non-work relationships, other than with immediate family members. This wasn't a problem when life was so full of interactions at work. But once that work door closed, my world felt very alone.

Fortunately, among the many upsides of transitioning is the opportunity to reset everything. This is the time to reclaim your life and relationships that matter to you, and/or pursue new relationships you may have lacked the bandwidth to enjoy in the past. It's a chance to eliminate unhealthy patterns that may have crept into your life.

With tremendous runway still ahead, you can redefine yourself and what you represent. It all starts with accepting that you cannot have it all figured out ahead of time—simply because you dedicated all of yourself to your job, advancing your career, fulfilling your employer's expectations.

Your Relationships with Family, Friends, and Faith

One of our clients, Pamela, enjoyed a tremendously successful career as a Financial Services executive. As she navigated her transition, she was grateful for the opportunity to be reflective and intentional about where to spend her time, and choiceful about what she focused on.

As I stepped away from my career, cancer had rocked my family. I had lost my father the year before, and both my mother and brother-in-law were battling long-term diagnoses. They ultimately passed away within weeks of each other. After moving in with my mother for six months—at her side nearly 24/7—I was physically and emotionally exhausted. Not having a partner or kids, I sometimes wished I had someone to enjoy coffee with in the morning, someone to be a sounding board for talking through this tremendous change. Instead, I leaned on three "F's" in my life—Family, Friends, and Faith—to find a very fulfilling Next Season.

Family. When I retired, I immediately moved into caregiver mode for my mom. The intensity was all-consuming, but my family was amazing. My sister would call to say, "Are you taking care of yourself?" Or my other sister would sense something was off and ask, "How can I help?" After we navigated through that incredibly difficult period, I felt that I could finally decompress and enjoy myself. A big part of that was becoming deeply involved with my niece's two little boys, who call me "AP" (Aunt Pamela). During the pandemic, I became part of the nanny brigade, which completely changed my life. I love being their "AP" more than I ever could have imagined.

Friends. I had to make and nurture friendships because I moved a gazillion times, starting in kindergarten, then attending schools in six different states before college. I have dear friends all over the country who I would drop everything for. (Their kids call me AP too!) Two years before retiring, I moved to another new city for work, where I ultimately made wonderful connections that would help keep my head in the game post-career. I joined a local women's resource group that invests in the community, figuring I could find some friends out of the 450 members—and I did!

Faith. While a strong spiritual faith is incredibly important to me, I realized that I also needed to tap into the faith I have in myself. Moving so many times helped me develop incredible adaptability and resiliency. These skills have been central to my Next

Season—appreciating the journey and rolling with its twists and turns. I've given myself permission to explore, try, fail, and succeed, and I am more fulfilled because of it.

Your Spouse/Partner Has a Next Season Too!

Leaders in transition often fail to recognize that their spouse/partner experiences stressors of the same magnitude, regardless of whether the significant other works outside or inside the home.

It's a huge transition for both of you, because your cadence and rhythms are incredibly disrupted. Active listening, empathy, and encouragement need to flow generously in both directions. It is essential that both parties be part of your Next Season planning.

It is especially important at this stage to recognize the myriad other roles that your spouse/partner has undertaken, separate from you. They have had to be highly independent and self-sufficient, creating their own lives that are active, productive, and fulfilling, completely separate from you.

So, a career transition impacts both of you individually. The clarity of purpose, rules of the journey, and destination are all reset with this transition. For some, new fears emerge about how decisions will be made, what life will look like posttransition, how each of you will adjust and find new rhythms.

The single action found to be most universally helpful at this juncture is to *talk about the transition.* Identify your concerns, both of you. Identify your hopes and dreams. Discuss options. Be open when things are working or not working. Keeping lines of communication wide open is critical to your successful transition.

Several leaders mentioned how helpful it was to have a project that they could work on together prior to formal retirement (such as building a new or second home). Rich, a former private company President & CEO, offers valuable insights on the essential spouse partnership:

After working in public policy for 17 years and the corporate world for another 20, I'm now ready for what my wife and I call "Life 3.0." I'd been working with my board leadership for five years on a strong succession plan, so I knew they were in good hands when time came for me to leave. When most people think about what they want to do after retirement, they think of their individual self. But for anyone who has a life partner, these decisions are for both of you. It is very important that your significant other plays the role they want and deserve in your plans moving forward. My advice:

Do your research. *My wife and I talked to a dozen couples and read several books as we looked forward to our retirement. Many suggested that we "hit the pause button" and take a sabbatical to refocus. So, we're going to take 3 to 6 months off, do some traveling, and refocus on the things we want to pursue in "Life 3.0."*

Embrace spontaneity. *As I was about to retire, I was asked to lead a year-long civic project that was very important to our region and our state, so we pushed back our sabbatical. It's been an enriching experience but required flexibility with respect to our initial plan.*

Focus on your faith. *My wife and I find our faith very important. It drives our lives, so we're using our newfound time to engage more in faith-based causes, in prayer, and in studying scripture.*

Leverage your strengths. *My wife and I have different strengths and weaknesses. But working as one team in this new phase of life, we can work as a more effective pair. I am called to be in a supportive role as she leads from her strengths.*

Don't be afraid to say no. *When you are approached with offers for things to do in your Next Season, many will be appealing and tempting. Don't be afraid to say no to things that don't fit your schedule and priorities. Be discerning about your choices and recognize that you are seeking the "best yes."*

A "PARTNER" Framework

Like many things in life, we have found it helpful to have a structure for conversation about the future to ensure that the dreams and concerns of both of you are considered in the planning phase. We offer the acronym PARTNER as a framework to guide your conversations and early planning efforts. (A more detailed version of this framework is in "Your Next Season Tools" at the back of the book.)

Priorities	*What priorities and goals do we have for this Next Season?*
Alternatives	*What alternatives do we have in how we spend our time?*
Realities	*What current realities/constraints do we have to work within?*
Togetherness	*What things do we want to achieve together?*
Non-togetherness	*What things do we wish to pursue independently?*
Events and actions	*What are our actions/next steps?*
Revisiting our plan	*When will we revisit our plan to see how we are doing?*

The silver lining of your Next Season, beyond just hairlines, is that this is a time for each of you to pursue passions you have kept at bay while you have lived for your work. This timing presents opportunities for both of you to make a difference in things or people you care about through your presence and engagement in areas for which you lacked bandwidth before.

Whether through volunteering for a non-profit, mentoring others, being more present for neighbors, friends, and family members, or at last pursuing dreams and desires, this is a season of unlimited possibilities in a world with great needs. Remember, though, that it is your Next Season for Two—the two of you together. Spouses/partners need to be front and center in the Next Season contemplations and planning—from the very start.

Alan Kelly

Previous Role: Vice President, ExxonMobil & President, Marketing

Retirement Date: 2016

Next Season Passions:
- MyNextSeason Advisor
- Entrepreneur/Philanthropist
- Devoted Family Man
- Music & Arts Lover

We were ready—together

On the exact day I retired, my wife and I also celebrated our 35th wedding anniversary. We'd had 35 great years living an international corporate lifestyle and had guided our children toward their own independent lives. It was a lovely natural milestone and the next phase for us as a couple. We were very excited.

A new schedule . . .

The biggest surprise was no alarm clock going off on Monday morning. We realized we weren't on somebody else's schedule. Immediately blessed with time, we started thinking deeply about the execution of our plan. We had already decided we would relocate to Colorado and build a mountain home. So, we had an immediate project to look forward to.

. . .and new priorities

My wife Carol had the idea to create a yellow board with Post-it notes on it that defined our priorities and our timelines. This has been really helpful because it allowed us to structure our thinking, move forward with immediate plans, and say no or not yet in a polite way to opportunities that didn't align with our goals. Our board has been our compass, if you will, our North Star. At the end of each year, we reflect on the yellow board and say, "Is this still right?"

Put the tech down and talk

Life is becoming more blurred because of technology, and it can get in the way of important conversations. It's more productive to sit down and talk about what

It's really important to have a partner who shares your values, supports you, and is willing to adapt to all the stresses of work and life."

your priorities are and how you will explore options both together and separately. If you're not talking to each other, if you're not sharing your stresses and your goals and your hopes, things tend to go off in separate directions.

Rekindle friendships

You have to be proactive in building or rebuilding relationships. It doesn't just happen. That first year after I

retired from ExxonMobil, we cultivated and renewed old friendships again. We devoted at least 12 months to reflecting on our priorities and traveling the world to spend time with the people that we really know and love—our family and our friends. Those relationships have all blossomed. For instance, I spent three weeks with a lifelong school friend and we recorded our first music album. We've been playing guitar since we were 12 years old, and we've always wanted to record an album, so we did it. That friendship means the world to me.

Avoiding overcommitment

I'm finding a lot of the coaching and advice I'm giving as a MyNextSeason advisor is on time management—a lesson Carol and I learned from our own journey. We didn't realize how much our commitments would expand. We said, "Let's open a local art gallery, that would be cool. We'll hire a manager, and we'll get it going." But even if you think "I'm going to step back and delegate," you tend to get pulled into day-to-day items that are very time consuming. So, be careful. Go in with full knowledge that things can become much more demanding than you imagine. We are very passionate about doing things we care about, so the risk grows that we take on too much.

Have an exit plan

Priorities shift. All three of our children were married during the first five years of our retirement and we had three grandchildren born. We had an aging parent in the UK. So, we began reassessing commitments to make time for these new responsibilities. We have had wonderful experiences running our gallery, giving back to community causes, and managing real estate projects. Stepping back from things also takes careful planning—something we underestimated.

The next, Next Season

We are calling our next phase "simplification" because we had expanded our lives to an extent where we felt like we were back in the fast lane. Simplification included the downsizing of our mountain home, the sale of a commercial property, and the closure of our art gallery. While maintaining our Colorado connections, we're planning to relocate near the heart of our family on the East Coast where there are also world-class medical facilities—an emerging priority for us as we age.

> **"**
> *We are calling our next phase "simplification" because we had expanded our lives to an extent where we felt like we were back in the fast lane."*

More time for simple joys

We're at that very privileged position of watching our children's families grow, which gives us incredible joy. But there are simple things as well. Singing in the choir gives Carol goosebumps when they're all on the stage. I still enjoy writing songs and playing Scrabble together in the evening or planning new travel adventures.

The power of partnership

It's really important to have a partner who shares your values, supports you, and is willing to adapt to all the stresses of work and life. Carol is my best friend. She's really been a mentor to me since I left the professional world because she has wonderful values. My relationship with her is important not only as wife, mother of our children, and best friend, but also as a guide.

8

Reactivating Old Muscles

....

Think about old relationships/connections
in new ways

No one knows better than you do that relationships are the key to success. That applies to both your career and your Next Season. Just as your network was essential in your career, your network is again essential as you think about your purpose and how to spend your time. You need your network to bounce ideas off of, explore areas of focus, and ultimately find what you want to do.

Most roles—whether on a board, not-for-profit volunteering, teaching, mentoring, or consulting—will come from your network. The future is all about relationships that matter, and connecting with people who can be a helpful bridge to things that interest you.

Networking is one of our previously most-used muscles, well-trained and sculpted in our early-career days. As we become more senior in our jobs, our "networking muscles" atrophy and we get lazy. We become accustomed to people seeking us out everywhere we go because of our positional power and status in the company or community.

This is one area of significant change when you transition. You will have fewer regular instances of being the magnet to which all the nails are automatically pulled. Rather, you will now need to use your magnetism to purposefully and proactively connect with others.

How Do You Reactivate Your Networking Muscle?

It starts with the phrase we know so well: *It's all about who you know.*

It's amazing how extensive each of our networks is when we really think about it. Friends. Family. Current or former customers. Parents of our children's friends you used to talk with on the sidelines at games and plays and concerts. The community attached to your in-laws, all of whom you met at "the wedding." You really know a LOT of people, and each one is connected to other people, organizations, and interesting possibilities.

Those organic connections are the perfect place to kickstart your networking plan.

John, a leader of a large corporation, shared these thoughts:

People always think of me as an extrovert, but in reality, I'm an introvert. I was interested in being on a board of directors and understood the importance of networking, but I really didn't know how to begin. I was headed to London for a week, so my Advisor and I put together a very simple plan to reach out and ask five former colleagues and friends to get together for coffee or lunch. These were people I enjoyed being around and genuinely wanted to reconnect with. I also trusted their advice and wanted to discuss my retirement ideas with them, including being on a board. I loved getting together with each of them so much that I replicated the process with friends and colleagues in my hometown and throughout the world.

"Networking" Doesn't Have to Be a Four-Letter Word

What's your reaction when someone suggests that you network? Many associate an overwhelming dread with this term—fear of the unknown, having to ask others for help—an uncomfortable vulnerability.

We often hear clients say, "I don't like networking. I don't even like the word, because it sounds so transactional." Well, okay . . . but as you think about networking, look for ways to make meaningful connections, reconnect with friends and colleagues, and build new relationships. Look for opportunities to learn and help those you are networking with. Networking done correctly is more than transactional—it's relationship-building!

Connecting Is the New Networking: Gary's Advice

Gary Frey, a friend of MyNextSeason, knows a thing or two about networking. Gary has held impressive roles within large and small companies, including founding a brand consultancy firm and serving as Chief Impact Officer at a PE/wealth planning firm, President of BizJournals.com, and SVP at Bank of America. But amid much success, Gary experienced great loss and hardship and had to redirect his career path many times. He is where he is today because of what he calls "connecting," as opposed to "networking."

While in Ohio with no job on the horizon, Gary and his wife thought: "Why not look for a job in Charlotte, NC, where we want to live?" Gary traveled to Charlotte, not necessarily to network but to reconnect with friends and hopefully build new relationships.

He began by asking friends to help him "make some meaningful connections," and from that simple request to a handful of people, his network grew exponentially. After more visits to Charlotte, filled with many introductions, quick meetups, and thoughtful conversations, Gary received a job offer on the last day of his third trip.

It is tempting to want a formula for networking or connecting. Gary's approach is more holistic, and above all is other-centric, rather than self-centric. His story suggests a mentality and motivation behind networking that is more intent on relationship-building than self-improvement. Here are his points to consider as you reconstruct your own networking foundation:

- **View your meetings as opportunities to build relationships.** Networking activities are often transactional and seem to be a means to an end, but don't view them that way. Instead, what can you learn from those you meet?

- **Connect with other connectors.** Create a list of personal contacts who know you, and could potentially connect you to others. (From the 20 people I initially contacted in Charlotte, I was able to connect to others to generate 90 meetings in a 6-week span!) If you lack your own network, seek help from a trusted friend who has one.

- **Get outside yourself and ask how you can help others.** It is natural to be self-consumed when networking. But instead of walking into a meeting thinking, "I hope this lands me a job," let your motivation be to help the other person. Not only does this make a better impression; it's a reminder to you that others have concerns beyond your goals.

- **Don't be pigeonholed.** If you see people limiting their search for you based on your previous work experience or the last job they know you had, it's up to you to reshape the conversation. Share your vision for your next role and your related strengths. For example:

  - "As you know, I've been *<insert most recent positions>* and am looking for the next thing. Here are a few things I'm looking for . . . "

- **Never miss an opportunity, even a doubtful one.** When a friend/contact suggests you meet with one of their contacts, always do so, even if you don't think it will serve you. You never know what will come from it! (I was hesitant to meet with a few contacts along the way, but one of those uncertain contacts eventually led to a job offer.)

- **Make it easy for those you are meeting.** Go to them. Buy their coffee, breakfast, lunch. (Dinner is often off the table because people want to be with their families, though meeting for a drink after work might work.)

- **State your "ask" early in the conversation.** Don't directly ask for a job, but rather share your interest, work history, passions, strengths. Make it clear why you're there and don't beat around the bush.

  - When it feels right, say something like, "As you get to know me, does anything resonate? Do you know of anybody I should know? If so, will you connect me?"

  - Also, be sure to ask, "Is there anything I can do for you?"

- **Enjoy yourself!** Enjoy the interesting people you meet and new opportunities to connect. There will be positive surprises along the way—watch for them and enjoy!

Networking Can Be Easier Than You Think

There are many ways to naturally network or connect, both while you are still working and post-transition. It doesn't have to be laborious and can easily involve established interests. Opportunities include:

- **Your alma mater.** Join alumni chapters or advisory groups.

- **Continuing membership with associations** in your industry or area of interest.

- **Local groups who share your interest areas.** Consider your community, Chamber of Commerce, YMCA, or place of worship.

- **Take up a cause,** one which has a natural community of interest.

- **Online groups.** Explore those for any area of interest, like LinkedIn.

- **Blogs and articles.** It's amazing what's out there!

Networking can be done in person, through social media, LinkedIn, email, and of course old-fashioned phone calls. It can mean reconnecting with an old colleague or friend, or reaching out to someone you'd like to get to know. It's not hard, but does require taking time to be intentional.

How Do You Stay Current, Connected, Relevant?

Many of our clients find it essential and stimulating to stay connected with prior coworkers, or regularly connect with friends for intellectually interesting conversations. It not only nurtures community and deepens friendships but feeds their desire to "stay connected to the business world."

One client, James, was treasurer of a large financial institution. Upon retiring, he felt a void, missing regular conversations that challenged his thinking and tapped his years of experience and wisdom. So he proactively set up a monthly breakfast with some professional peers, two of whom were still working full time at his prior employer. And he shared the rewarding result with us:

This sounds like a setup for a joke! An economist, a head of credit, a line-of-business leader, and I walk into a breakfast bar. We do this monthly for about 1½ hours. First, we spend 10–15 minutes talking about our families. Then we discuss the economy, the market, what we're investing in, and the political landscape. We each do our homework before meeting and stay up-to-speed in our areas of expertise.

These breakfasts give us the opportunity to engage with each other, feel and enjoy community, and stay intellectually challenged. It's a fun way to preserve our valuable relationships. And we continue to learn so much from each other!

Now, Go Flex That Muscle!

Nearly all the leaders we have advised and interviewed underscored the importance of networking while they were still in their roles (ideally), and most certainly afterward. They surprised themselves with the extent of their networks and the enjoyment they found in reconnecting with people and making new professional acquaintances.

Think outside the box as you contemplate who might be interesting to connect with or meet, and how you can make it happen. Thankfully, you can easily tap into your muscle memory for networking and find the experience both professionally and personally rewarding.

Laura Hay

Previous Role: KPMG Global Head of Insurance

....

Retirement Date: 2023

....

Next Season Passions:
- Fortune 100 Board Director
- Not-for-Profit Board Director
- Women's Leadership Advocate

It's no secret I'm a planner

At KPMG, my retirement date was fixed, so I knew the time-line for years. I had so many things I couldn't wait to do!

I loved serving on the KPMG Board, so I wanted similar work in retirement. My transition was ten years out, so when I started to look into it, I was told I was eight years too early! But that didn't stop me from thinking about it.

Charting a path

So many people asked what I planned to do that I developed a pie chart with four quadrants: Family & Travel, Women's Leadership, Boards & Service, and Theater & Arts. (In college, I couldn't decide whether to be an actress or an actuary.) When I showed it to my doctor, she said, "Where's Self-Care?" So, I added a Self-Care circle in the middle because it was central to making all my goals happen.

A variety of fulfillments

A corporate board was one piece of my retirement plan, but not my *whole* plan. I decided my life's work was to develop and promote future female leaders. I launched "Mind the Gap," a blog that had over three million views, and I ran workshops worldwide on confidence and risk-taking—for the sole purpose of paying it forward. I didn't want that to stop when I retired, so I joined a regional Girl Scouts not-for-profit board to continue my passion for empowering women and girls. I also take every leadership speaking engagement I can.

Networking has been key to all of my opportunities, which means being organized and diligent, recognizing the focus and energy it involves, and not waiting for it to come to me."

Making it happen

To make my pie chart a reality, especially Boards & Service, I needed to be more organized in networking and relationships. I started with a list of board members, C-Suite executives, and organizations of interest I could talk to. I created a list of questions, always ending the conversation with "Do you have anybody else you'd suggest I speak to?" Sometimes people would say no, but many would offer a warm hand-off to another person. Following this strategy during the two years before my retirement led to 150+ conversations.

Connect outside your orbit

If you network with those in your immediate orbit, you'll just hear about the same opportunities. Indeed, I learned that many who land board seats did so through "weak" or "loose" relationships. So, even if I felt nervous, I got very aggressive about reaching out to people I didn't know.

Treat advice like feedback

I've always felt that advice is a gift, and I treat it like feedback. To anybody feeling bombarded by it, just be open to hearing it—it doesn't mean you have to take it. I sought maximum advice and wrote it all down, even if it didn't feel relevant. You never know when it might be useful.

I've revisited that advice and later thought, "Oh my gosh, that's right on point!"

Stay in control

A recruiter once aggressively wanted me to interview during a certain week. I didn't have time to think about the company, and it didn't go well. I learned to give myself time to prepare for a great interview, which means doing it when it works for me, not for everybody else. I'm a preparer, and this interviewing takes more preparedness! Board seats don't come up every day—you want to ensure you're giving it your best shot.

Landing a Fortune 100 Board

I'm now on the board of MetLife, and networking played a big role in getting there. One of my former clients had transitioned to board work, and I stayed in touch. When I was about two years from retirement, I arranged dinner with him, and asked, "I'm about to start looking for boards. Any advice?" He offered to make introductions at MetLife.

I had more than ten interviews, and my MyNextSeason Advisor guided me on explaining the value and skills I could bring to their board. I was announced in February 2024, and I'm both excited and proud! But the real story is how it all started with relationships!

Networking toward joy

Ten years before I retired, I already knew the importance relationships would have in achieving my goals. But the unexpected blessing was that networking to land on a board developed into relationships for living my life. It's not about having every next step planned—it's about finding your joy and leaning into it.

9

Your Plan

....

100% structure with 100% flexibility

You have created countless plans throughout your career: strategic plans, implementation plans, growth plans. Plans to divest, plans to acquire. And the strength of each plan, when reviewed 6 or 12 months later, was whether it held up through the test of time and whether it followed relatively unchanged from its original design.

However, your new "transition plan" (which we will now call *Your Plan*) shares few characteristics with those others you spent your career developing, evaluating, and implementing! In fact, a great transition plan evolves with time and learnings, and rarely stays the same when evaluated 6 or 12 months later.

We encourage you to adopt 100% structure with 100% flexibility. It is important to have a structured, specific plan. But it is equally important to be flexible and evolve your plan, or even change it completely as post-transition events and relationships unfold. You need to have options and be able to adapt to whatever comes your way.

In fact, we encourage using "modifiers" when you answer the many questions about what you will do next. As we shared previously, our favorites are "For now," or "Right now," which alert you and your contacts that your Next Season will be defined by changing characteristics, versus a single title/role/ affiliation . . . and that change/transitioning is an integral part of Your Plan.

Some Wise Counsel from Our Colleagues and Clients

One colleague, Jim, was Executive Vice Chairman and CFO of an international corporation. He felt intensely about the importance of planning:

My company mandated retirement age, so I knew when I'd retire years ahead of the actual date. I thought a lot about what I wanted to do, but ultimately the "where" trumped the "what." My wife and I wanted to move across the country to a warmer climate, so I decided not to look for new possibilities until we found a new home. Eventually I got both. Here's my advice:

- *Plan!* *You plan for every other phase of life, so make sure you also plan for this new phase—especially the non-financial aspects. Start with something basic, like where you'd like to live or whether you want to work full time, part time, and/or give back to a not-for-profit. Making those initial decisions helps make settling on the specifics much easier.*

- *There are multiple phases of retirement.* *After moving and settling in, I began working for a private equity firm and traveling a lot for them. But after a few years I transitioned into a more leisurely lifestyle.*

- *Help the organizations that helped you.* *My college years were extremely formative for me, so I decided to give back to the school by serving on some of their committees and helping to fundraise.*

- *Use your free time to travel.* *If you can afford it, travel with your entire family. We've thoroughly enjoyed spending time away with our kids and grandkids. You'll make memories that will last a lifetime.*

- *Stay active.* *Be disciplined about engaging in things that interest you and learning new things.*

- *Take advantage of the control you now have.* The best part of being retired is channeling your skills and abilities in whatever direction you want. You get to manage your schedule. You get to decide what you do and when.

- *Make two lists.* Name one "Productive Things I Want to Do," and the other "Fun Things I Want to Do." You'll be surprised by how many overlap!

Planning begins with a closer self-examination, which we explored in Chapter 3, "The Pause to Discern." From this you can begin to formulate your plan for your Next Season.

All well and good, but what if your timetable is abruptly accelerated? A former Chief Human Resources Officer for an international corporation, who prided himself on careful career planning, was caught off-guard—without a plan for his retirement transition. He offers this advice:

I spent my entire career having a game plan. I was deliberate in strategizing each move, never leaving anything to chance. I always knew what needed to be done. However, I didn't have a plan for how I would spend my time during retirement, because I thought it would be a natural transition: "I'm passionate about everything, so I'll just find other things." Well, retirement came abruptly, and there was no soft landing. My advice:

- *Plan your retirement.* Process this upcoming Next Season before it arrives. Don't wait until you're already retired to figure it out. There are emotional ramifications that come when you lack a plan!

- *Engage in mentally challenging/stimulating activities.* Know what you need. You've been living in a challenging landscape for most of your life, and to lose this altogether can be extremely disheartening.

- *Set realistic goals before retirement.* If you're thinking you'll start an abundance of new hobbies/activities post-retirement, *think again. If you are not already incorporating such interests into your life now, you probably won't in retirement.*

- **Schedule time to see people regularly.** *Be intentional about extending invitations to people with whom you wish to be connected.*

- **Spend your new time with those you love.** *I have gotten to spend more time with my grandchildren, and it has been wonderful.*

- **Anticipate the changes ahead—physically, emotionally, and mentally.** *Give yourself space and time to adjust to this new lifestyle and to feel the normal ups and downs of transition. Be gracious with yourself—you've earned it!*

We at MyNextSeason strongly agree: have a game plan for retirement. For a successful transition, you need a plan—for day 1, week 1, year 1. Of course, don't overschedule or perpetuate an unhealthy overcommitment. But you need to have things on the calendar. And remember, just because you have a plan, it's not set in stone—stay flexible.

Kathy, a former Fortune 20 EVP, offered this reflection and advice on transition planning:

My transition was wonderfully smooth because I spent a lot of time planning. After 30 years of traveling for business, I was ready for a change in lifestyle. I gave my company 10 months' notice so that I could finish well and have time to plan MyNextSeason. My advice:

- **Create a departure plan.** *Spend your final six months on the job preparing to leave so you can end well. Have a plan for the nine months following your transition so you can start well and have some structure in place.*

- **Create a written plan for things you want to do during retirement.** *This is sort of a bucket list for this chapter of your life.*

- **Define a purpose for your Next Season.** *Going in, I knew I wanted to spend more time with my family, spend time volunteering, and spend time going back to school to learn some things I had always wanted.*

- **Take advantage of where you live.** *Explore your city and neighborhood.*

- **If you traveled a lot for business,** *plan a few vacations so you can cure your restlessness and experience travel in a whole new way.*

- **Flexibility is the best part.** *I've gotten to spend more time with my family and have a lot more time for self-reflection and doing things I have long wanted to do, but never had the time.*

- **Sample things before you commit.** *I tried out a number of volunteer opportunities before picking a few I wanted to stick with.*

- **Ask others for advice.** *Whether it be a transition advisor or a friend who has traveled this road before you, they can be helpful. Be open to their willingness to help.*

- **Adjust the elements of your life to fit your new structure.** *I rearranged my closet and office to fit my new role as a student and volunteer, versus being an executive.*

- **Be willing to try new things.**

- **Don't shortcut the planning.** *It's the most important part!*

At the end of the day, the skills you acquire through your job and career are those you will have wherever you go. Wherever you can use those skills as a true asset, is where you can deploy your time and talents. Some have likened their next phase of life to a project they are passionate about . . . something that can be planned ahead, executed at whatever desired pace, with whomever they choose, and with the ability to make changes and adjustments at any time.

Never wake up asking yourself what you are going to do. Rather, wake up excited for the things you plan to do—even if it's just reading three newspapers, walking with a friend, taking your pet to the vet, or meeting friends for drinks and dinner.

Sometimes it takes a physical move to a different dwelling or new area to prompt/encourage new patterns of behavior. Many of our clients have tried long-term (temporary) rentals in new communities with closer access to things they love, plus opportunities to meet more people in the same phase of life. Others report that building a new home as a family project was engaging and bonding at the beginning of their Next Season. It gave them a project to work on together and a shared investment in their future.

One executive cautions of the risk of moving too far outside of your skill set. He was intrigued with becoming a commercial arbitrator. Some influential legal friends in that field had observed his ability to negotiate remedies from legal actions and encouraged him. So, in the years prior to his retirement, he worked hard to establish contacts in this new field and was encouraged that it would work out. However, in the end, he discovered that his skill set was not distinctive enough to compete with the many judges already in that space.

The silver lining was that, in the process, he found that advisory work drew on his experience in a different working context. It gave him the best of both worlds—a fresh perspective leveraging the experience he had gained over his career. And so he pivoted to pursue advising, leaving the world of commercial arbitration to others. Note that this executive got to this new place by exploring new interests!

There are no shoulds or right answers when it comes to Your Plan. Just create a plan to guide you and your priorities in the early days—especially until you figure out what you truly want to do in your first Next Season.

We See These Consistent Top Three Priorities

In our first ten years of interviewing leaders post-transition, we noted strong consistency among the top three priorities in Next Season plans:

1. **Spending time with family and friends.** Nearly every leader prioritized closing the gap between *time* spent with family and *value* placed on family. An interesting observation: in a world of two-career families, grandparents who lived nearby seized the opportunity to be an integral part of their grandchildren's lives. The working parents had to miss many activities and events, so the grandparents filled in, joyfully. Also, many interviewees put a financial priority on paying for family travel to be together. They demonstrated that priority by enabling it for their younger children/families.

2. **Becoming more physically active.** All leaders recognized the importance of a healthier lifestyle, and desired to make this a high priority in allocating time and energy. Related: several also mentioned obtaining the best medical advice as a key to their future.

3. **Spending time in areas where you have purpose.** For some, this included teaching, coaching, board work, or not-for-profit work, Others spoke of wanting to use their domain-specific skills to help either individuals or organizations, where needed.

Corporate leaders recognized that their hard-learned organizational skills are badly needed in the not-for-profit world. Some leaders reported early experiences with not-for-profits that led to important choices.

However, many expressed frustration with their not-for-profit engagements: limited resources, poor management, inefficiencies. These led our clients to be selective in choosing a not-for-profit, choosing organizations whose causes tugged at their heartstrings or for which they felt passion.

Eli, a former Fortune 100 VP, chose to retire because he wanted a change:

I retired because I wanted something new and different. So, I gave 10 months' notice and began my Next Season. For a few months, I just relaxed, but also sought new ways to use the skills and expertise gained during my career. So, I transitioned into consulting, and then to business startups. I was a founding principal of a business accelerator that brings management talent and seed financing to emerging technologies. This was an exciting new way to use my skills. Retiring doesn't mean you have to be done working! If you enjoy what you are doing, it isn't really working anyway. My advice:

- **Leaving a corporate position can be a dramatic change.** *After living within a certain routine for years, transitioning to something new can be daunting. Mentally preparing can make everything easier.*

- **Make plans and have goals, but don't put on blinders.** *Move into your Next Season with forethought, but be open to new experiences and opportunities that might not arrive until after your transition.*

- **Take the opportunity to volunteer.** *Since leaving my corporate position, I've had more time to serve at my church and on the board of a local museum, both of which have been rewarding.*

- **Do what you want, when you want.** *That's the best part about being retired. Don't paint yourself into a box with too many commitments right away.*

- **Meet interesting people and open new doors.** *The world is full of them. Take advantage of both in your Next Season.*

- *Write down your goals and review them. This can help you stay on track. Having a concrete mission can help you avoid saying "yes" to things you will regret later.*

- *Take time to think and relax before jumping into your Next Season. When you retire, people want to know how you plan to spend your time, but don't be in a hurry to answer that question.*

Companies provide a platform for talented leaders to use their gifts and talents. They use, reuse, refine, stretch—and sometimes overuse—those muscles to benefit the company, its people, and its business.

With a transition to your Next Season, those gifts and talents stay with you—always. It's just the company platform you leave behind. Part of your new plan is deciding who will be the next beneficiaries of your amazing talents, bruises, learnings, and gifts.

Burnet Tucker

Previous Role: Global Head of Leadership Development & Learning, Bank of America

Retirement Date: 2015

Next Season Passions:
- MyNextSeason Advisor
- Leadership Coach
- Not-for-Profit Board Director

Insecurities of exiting

I had been very involved in my own succession plan. But after I left BofA, I still had these surprising, unsettling feelings about how easily the organization seemed to replace me. And how they moved on so successfully without me. I wondered how well I would have been performing if I had stayed. Rationally, things running well didn't mean my 25 years brought no value, or that I was incapable of achieving what they were doing now. But emotionally I had to learn how to stop assessing my performance in a job that I no longer had. I could not let feelings of self-doubt detract from my overall sense of worth. BofA's continued success was not my own failure.

The power of the pause

As an HR executive, I was famously structured and organized. But when I decided to retire, I had no set plan for my future, which shocked everyone who knew me. I was confident in my decision, but unsure of what was next. Shortly after my departure, I had the opportunity to experience the MyNextSeason executive transition program. I began working with an Advisor to discern what my next phase would look like. My Advisor encouraged me to take "the pause."

So I gave myself 6 months to do "nothing," and it was pivotal for me. It not only freed me from pondering my next steps, but also from holding myself to performance and productivity measures. I didn't have to engage in new things just to feel I was accomplishing something. I traveled and spent a lot of time with my family. And after my hiatus, my Next Season plan started to grow organically.

> Building a Next Season in which I am intentional with my time has allowed me to put my energy into new and, sometimes, unexpected joys."

Trading expectations for authenticity

I wanted to find a new way to use my skills and experience, but without my former intensity and time commitment. I considered starting my own consulting business. It felt like everyone expected me to do that, and I think I expected it of myself. But the more I thought about it, I realized that "hanging my own shingle" wasn't for me. I didn't want to be a sole operator.

Finding a new fit

I realized that the most enjoyable part of my HR experience was coaching. I also saw tremendous benefit being a client to a MyNextSeason coach. Then MyNextSeason asked me to join their advising team, and it seemed like the right fit. Over the past several years, it has proven to be a great way to apply my coaching skills and be part of a supportive team.

Putting the rest together

The Burnet of 10 years ago would never have imagined she would one day be dressed in a beautiful sari, with tika on her head, participating in a Hindu religious festival! But now I've had that honor and so many other amazing experiences because I committed to pursuing causes I care about. In addition to coaching with MyNextSeason, I have served several not-for-profits in varying capacities.

For the past several years, my husband and I have participated in a program called Fruitful Friends, and we  have become close to a local refugee family from Nepal. At first I was hesitant, knowing it would require navigating cultural differences and a language barrier. But I am so glad that I was able to push out of my comfort zone and pursue this opportunity! It has led to rich cultural experiences and meaningful friendships. Building a Next Season in which I am intentional with my time has allowed me to put my energy into new and sometimes unexpected joys.

What's next

It's been 9 years, and I've done many incredible things that I could not have anticipated. Now I am moving on from some things I did shortly after retiring, and I am learning there is not just one Next Season for me. Hopefully there will be many more, as I keep exploring interests and refining my priorities. I will continue to help others through their own transitions as a MyNextSeason Advisor, but I'm also excited to dive into some new discernment about what I might want my next, Next Season to look like!

10

Achieving Purpose

Find purpose in all your actions and time

Perhaps the most important criterion for a successful Next Season is feeling that *you found purpose* in what you do, and how you spend your time. You are greeted with a transition from *have* to do, to *want* to do—and with that comes immense freedom and choice in how you will spend your time.

As George Bernard Shaw observed—

> *This is the true joy in life, the being used for a purpose recognized by yourself as a mighty one . . . the being a force of Nature instead of a feverish, selfish little clod of ailments and grievances complaining that the world will not devote itself to making you happy.*

As Shaw implies, the gift of this season is the time to choose how you spend your time, energy, and expertise. Many leaders find their purpose through engaging in things that mean the most to them: family, giving back, charitable causes that touch their heart—or that they feel the world needs some muscle behind.

Take Time to Really Contemplate Your Purpose

Purpose is different from goal, although they are often used interchangeably. A goal is a target, an end result. But your purpose is about your whole being, and understanding it requires generous time and space to consider:

What are you meant to do in your lifetime? Where are your gifts and capabilities best used in service to the greater world or others? What brings joy that you can feel from the top of your head to the tips of our toes? When do you feel the most proud, the most contributory, the most fulfilled?

These are the questions you explore when you examine your *purpose.*

When Ben, a former Fortune 10 VP, transitioned into his Next Season, he dramatically redefined his purpose:

I dedicated my Next Season to bringing electricity to remote communities in Africa. Doing this combined my faith, project management skills, and engineering expertise to change the lives of others—thus finding true purpose in my Next Season.

I always knew that, when I retired, I would find a way to give back. I had a plan in place, making my Next Season something I looked forward to. Now I'm using my engineering and project management skills to dramatically impact the lives of those less fortunate. Here's my advice:

- **Look to your past to inspire your future.** *My transition was about returning to work I had been unable to engage in full-time for years. Whether going back to school or resuming an old hobby, your Next Season can be a great time to revisit your past.*

- **Give back through not-for-profit work.** *There are so many people around the world who could benefit from your help. Find a way to lend a hand.*

- **Repurpose your old skills.** *I use the administrative and management skills I gained working for a corporation to more effectively lead a not-for-profit, even though those fields are very different.*

- **Assess your financial situation.** *Obviously, this will be high on your list as you consider your Next Season options.*

- *Enjoy the time with your family.* I have five children and several grandchildren I want to spend time with. So I make sure my life isn't so hectic that it cuts away from my time with them.

- *Plan and work toward your Next Season.* Your Next Season will not just happen, just like your career didn't just happen. You have to work hard and plan for this new chapter in your life, just as you did your previous chapters.

- *Figure out what you are passionate about.* What will satisfy you as you move forward? Make the most of this exciting new time in your life.

Another executive, Wayne, retired as a Director of a Fortune 100 industrial company. He wanted to give back in his Next Season. Like Ben, he felt a calling to do that after a successful corporate career:

I wanted to get involved with not-for-profits while I was working, but I traveled so much that I didn't have the time. After retiring, I got involved in a lot of efforts within my community, which is where I felt called. It meant a lot to me to give back in this way, and I found the activity and engagement with new people very enjoyable. My advice:

- *Anchor yourself outside of what you do at work.* This way your identity is not tied solely to what you do for a living. Take pride in the many roles you play. You're a lot more than your former job title.

- *Stay grounded when you are a CEO.* When your corporate perks go away, you will still have things to keep you happy and motivated.

- *Consider assisting your successor by serving as a consultant.* This is a great way to ease out of corporate life.

- *Manage everything with your spouse or partner.* In many cases, they struggle just as much as you do and need help transitioning as well.

- **Use your free time to leave a legacy to your children and grandchildren.** *One thing I'm doing for them is writing a book about where I've come from and what I've done.*

- **Enjoy your freedom.** *You get to do your own planning. Stay busy, but save time to relax.*

- **Find both a doctor and financial planner who are younger than you.** *This way you will have them for the long run.*

- **Be comfortable as the person you are.** *At parties, you are no longer an executive, but a grandfather and an active board member in your community.*

Tom, a former physician, found fulfillment in singing with the choir and praise band at his church. And he is grateful for more time to read without interruption. His advice:

- **The gifts of retirement are time and choice.** *Now I have plenty of time and the ability to choose my own ways to fill it.*

- **Don't retire without a plan.** *Are you going to put in time on a board, at church, at school, at a second job, or traveling? Don't retire without a plan. Have a clear place to spend your time.*

- **Enjoy new reading time.** *I've really enjoyed reading more during my Next Season. I have more time, and can spend hours with a book now, where before I could only read during brief snippets of time, if at all.*

- **Use your career skills in new ways.** *Since I was a doctor, I now volunteer with Hospice, which has impacted so many people during such a difficult time in their lives.*

- **Grow in your faith.** *If you are religious, use retirement as a time to grow. I've become a much stronger and more committed Christian during my Next Season.*

• **Improve your health.** *Spend time focusing on your physical health as well as your mental and spiritual health.*

In our work with leaders, four themes pinpoint what gave them the greatest sense of purpose in their Next Seasons:

1. Being intentional with how you spend your time

2. Having the flexibility to respond to unexpected opportunities of interest

3. Having presence with family and friends in meaningful and helpful ways

4. Giving back to causes you care about

By far, the most direct benefit of post-corporate life is having control over your time and your activities. Over and over, people cite reluctance to over-commit in retirement.

People also value having the capacity to respond to invitations, to explore interesting ideas and possibilities, and to engage in things of interest. Having capacity and availability in their schedule was something highly unfamiliar to most leaders.

Norman, a former Fortune 100 operating company president, found himself in retirement transition due to health. Unfortunately, his health also nullified his long-planned Next Season of building homes for persons in need. He continued the discernment process as he sought purpose for his Next Season, and found it: leading a not-for-profit focused on food security for the hungry.

Norm's insights inspire one to retain optimism—even if you face personal obstacles. He encourages us to maintain a relentless search for purpose in our Next Season.

When I had major back surgery, I decided it was time to retire. I had wanted to help build homes for those in need, but the surgery prevented this. So, I found a new and unexpected calling working for a not-for-profit. It helped me make my Next Season a produc-

tive one, allowing me to greatly contribute with the skills I had gained in the corporate world. It really consumed my days and nights—and how I spent my weekends. Through this effort, I felt like I was making a difference and giving back. My advice:

- **Don't just sit around—seek activity.** Being at home without a plan is not a sustainable way to spend retirement. Initially I followed the stock market on TV and bought groceries. Then I opened my eyes and really asked myself, "What will my Next Season be? What do I want to do?"

- **Businesspeople can really help not-for-profits.** Look for those that need your specific skill set and whose mission is an interest area or passion for you.

- **Spend more time with your loved ones.** Retirement is a great time to make memories for your children and grandchildren.

- **Plan activities for yourself.** Family is important, but everyone has their own individual schedules and lives. People think family, golf, and travel, but a lot of time you need something more to fill your days and give you purpose.

- **A well-thought-out retirement plan is paramount.** If you think you have it all figured out just by having a date to retire, you've already lost the battle. Put a lot of thought into the level of activity you want in your Next Season and where you specifically want to be involved.

- **Never underestimate your ability to make a difference.** A difference for, and with, people and populations who really need help.

One of our clients, Susan, offers the following perspective, and speaks to her finding purpose after transitioning from her role as a Fortune 50 senior executive. Her advice:

- **Repurpose your skills.** *Consider skills you have developed over your career, and how you might use them in a new way. I was able to transfer my skills in finance, strategic planning, due diligence, and mentoring into a new role as officer and board member of one of America's largest not-for-profits. The change is exciting, and I feel I am living into my purpose. It's also fulfilling to use skills I spent years developing.*

- **Plan both your career exit and your Next Season entrance.** *Before I retired, I agreed to deepen my service on a couple of non-profit boards. After I retired, I extended my volunteer work through my church and into education, both areas where I have tremendous passion. I consciously booked my time early on, doing things that were meaningful to me.*

- **Your new-found free time is not endless.** *It will be quickly absorbed by people and organizations who want to tap into your talents. Decide how you want to spend your time—and be comfortable saying "no" to things that fall outside what you see as your purpose.*

- **Resist temptation to continue your same work.** *Even if you think you want to continue to work, resist the temptation (or calls from search firms) to immediately jump back into doing the same thing at a different firm. Take time to really understand what you want your Next Season to look like.*

- **Strengthen and renew your friendships.** *Now that you have more time, develop your bonds with others. I rarely had the time to take a leisurely lunch or a long walk in the neighborhood with a good friend. It is a true gift now, and I try to embrace it as much as possible.*

It's hard to know when you have "achieved purpose." It is not black-and-white, and it looks different at different stages of life. As we have suggested throughout this book, your life post-career seems to mirror life in a broader context: seasons defined by different characteristics, which flow one into the other. It may be that your purpose evolves and changes with time, or that you live more deeply into it with time.

We found ourselves most inspired by the many, many, many leaders with whom we spoke, who saw their Next Season as an invitation to live more fully into their purpose.

Mark Shaiken

Previous Role: Former Senior Partner & Board Member, Stinson LLP

Retirement Date: 2019

Next Season Passions:
• Published Author
• Entrepreneur/Philanthropist
• Devoted Family Man

Leaving the law

I tell people that law school and practicing law are great for teaching how to be a lawyer and how to help clients. But there's no training whatsoever for how *not* to be a lawyer anymore! It's kind of scary. I had spent a fair amount of time thinking about retiring. I think almost every lawyer goes through that—it's just something that's on your mind. Am I going to do this for the rest of my life? Or is there something else that comes after?

Clean break vs. phasing out

I was pretty adamant: as a lawyer, I was either in or out. For somebody else, it might be fine to continue practicing, in a reduced manner. But I'm the type that, if I slowed down rather than fully stopped, I'd still work too much. It would still focus all my attention on work, taking away from the other things that I wanted to do.

Unexpected euphoria

Right after I retired, something unexpected happened. I instantly felt euphoric! Not because I finally got out of jail or something like that; after all, I loved my job (corporate bankruptcy attorney for over 38+ years) and my firm. But all of a sudden, endorphins were released in a humongous magnitude inside my brain, and suddenly everything could wait until tomorrow. That lasted about a month.

Once that started to wane, I proceeded to do the things I wanted to do, which has turned out to be writing books.

A life-long "what if"

I've always wanted to write. It just took an entire law career for me to see if I could really do it, or if it was a pipe dream! I find it very cool. I've now written five books, including my memoir and four fiction novels. Writing my memoir first was very helpful. It allowed me to pause, take a breath and realize how I got to where I was. Once I got that off my chest, I was ready to dive into fiction.

> *I've always wanted to write. It just took an entire law career for me to see if I could really do it, or if it was a pipe dream!"*

I had a lot of moments of "Are you out of your mind? You've never written fiction before!" But I powered through and I really enjoy the main character I've created. I have a great book designer and a great editor. I enjoy all the different parts of it. And I'm a lot better at it now!

Pursuing multiple passions

Sliding into retirement, I was already starting to do some of the things I hoped to do. I was, and still am, on the Audit Committee for Habitat for Humanity in Denver. I love that, especially since I'm not really able to get up on a ladder anymore. I also continue to pursue sports photography, which was a rewarding creative outlet for me while practicing law. (I think people wondered if I was a sports photographer who tried cases, or a lawyer who took pictures!) Hopefully, I have a few years left sitting cross-legged courtside. The University of Denver has given me some wonderful opportunities in the past few years, including covering a nationally ranked women's gymnastics program, a sport I'd never photographed before.

The benefit of guidance ...

Even though I had a plan for my retirement, I was so glad to have a MyNextSeason Advisor as a thought partner. He helped me stop focusing on retiring *from* the law and instead focus on retiring *to* something else. It turns out it's very easy not to be a lawyer anymore. You just stop. The second part is harder. I owe my Advisor a huge debt of gratitude.

> **"**
> *There isn't a cookie cutter answer. I only say that I am a living example that there isn't just one thing to do in life and be satisfied."*

... and the challenge of passing it along

After my memoir was published, I was invited to speak on career pivot podcasts, as if I had some actual expertise. I don't have any specific advice, other than it's doable. It certainly can be scary. But for me, planning helped manage the scariness. There isn't a cookie cutter answer. I only say that I am a living example that there isn't just one thing to do in life and be satisfied.

A new sense of self and happiness

People ask who you are at a cocktail party, and you say, "I'm a lawyer." But that's not really who you *are*. That's what you *do*. I have a better idea now of who I am. I don't have lawyer war stories anymore, but I'm OK with that. I'm not necessarily exactly where I planned, but about 95% of what I had thought would happen, really did. I'm pretty happy. I smile a lot. Lawyers don't always smile a lot, but I do now.

11

More Changing Seasons

....
Above all, have grace in your transitions

The only certainty is change. And as we grow older, more variables enter our lives, impacting how we feel and spend our time. Many leaders find themselves reliving their earlier years as parents when the needs of their grown children and/or aging parents consume a major part of daily life.

It could mean direct delivery of care and face-to-face contact, or not. Regardless, supporting those in your family who need it, and remaining nearby to do so, become powerful influencers of your decisions about where to live and where to spend time.

A Reflection on Next Seasons, Happy and Sad

Some seasons can be predicted and managed, but some are beyond our control. One of our MyNextSeason Advisors, Bill, tells his remarkable story of *four* Next Seasons:

....
My wife Judy and I had three Next Seasons prior to her cancer diagnosis and passing. Our experience revealed several themes that are predictable and can be anticipated:
- *Desire/ability for long-distance travel*
- *Presence of grandchildren*
- *Currency of career networks and experience*
- *Desire to be part of our local communities*

These can drive significant decisions. In our case, looking back over all three of our Next Seasons, each was driven by a specific need—

- Season One: Escaping from corporate life.
- Season Two: Reestablishing our Canadian roots.
- Season Three: Becoming participants in our son's family and grandson's lives.

Each of our Next Seasons had its own rhythm, and brought its own gifts. And now I am living my unanticipated fourth Next Season, with tremendous gratitude for Judy and all our life together involved, as I find joy again without her by my side.

Our first Next Season. We started planning a couple of years before I retired. Our centerpiece was a new home on a remote, beautiful beach on Grand Cayman. Judy and I had a lot of fun planning the details, even building a model ourselves. I mention this because the act of planning and building the model created a reality about our new life.

In my case, it was doubly important, because I was unable to retire as soon as I had expected, so planning kept us engaged in our future. The time also enabled me to start making contacts for my desired Next Season purpose: industrial arbitration.

Our first Next Season was all we had dreamed of. But it also came with the unexpected: our house was destroyed by a hurricane before we could occupy it (thank goodness my retirement was delayed)! And industrial arbitration turned out to be a bust for me. However, the house and location provided the complete break from the corporate world that I needed, and I discovered the world of leadership consulting. (I now have over two dozen fascinating clients!)

Our second Next Season. This one was about returning to our roots. We had lived all over the world, which was fascinating and rewarding. But along the way we seemed to have lost something important—our connections to home in Canada. We are fortunate to have our roots in a large family and a wonderful country. We felt that it was time to reconnect, and to give back.

So, in our second Next Season, we traded our house for a condo in Cayman, which we could more easily visit for part of the year and established a new home base in eastern Canada. We also discovered, like many others, that moving back home after so many years is not as easy as you might think. It took a lot of work to reestablish our network of business and family relationships.

It's humbling that my demanding global-scale job did not give me automatic access to the more closed world of those who have worked together their whole lives! It was also frustrating to be a "new" member at the golf club once again, after so many years—no matter how well I played! (Btw, not an advantage I could rely on!)

In our second Next Season, it again helped that we had anticipated it. We bought a condo and joined the golf club well in advance and engaged our family in anticipating our return. I was greatly helped by old friends who encouraged me to join a couple of think tanks where my international experience was highly valued.

Our third Next Season. This was marked by arrival of our grandson. We, like many others, were surprised by the marked change in our priorities—to become a more integral part of our immediate family. In parallel, my interests shifted toward legacy issues—a collaboration with my brother on our family history and building a national discussion about what is distinctive about being Canadian.

In our early seventies, we decided to build our dream home on 17 acres, looking over the Gulf islands off British Columbia's coast. Many of our friends thought we were nuts! But we were exercising again those muscles of making a new life, actually participating in the life of our grandson, and having the fun of building the house we had dreamed of for 50 years!

Sadly and unexpectedly, that house also became the place Judy would live out her final years, ultimately losing a fiercely-fought battle with cancer.

__This loss ushered in my fourth Next Season.__ In this one, I was alone and searching. But a year after Judy's passing, I committed to reinvigorate my life with travel, new relationships, and finding joy again. By the grace of God, I met a wonderful woman, Annie, who was similarly widowed. We had much in common, and suddenly, I was in a new season with a sense of joy that had eluded me for quite some time. So, I guess I am in my fifth Next Season now, gratefully married to Annie, excited to live out the rest of our days together, and utterly thankful to have found someone who showed me there is light beyond the darkness.

Just as we transition from winter to spring, we know that summer and fall will come, too. The circle of life ensures this. And with it come transitions in our own lives. Above all, it is important to have grace in these transitions. Grace, first and foremost toward yourself, as you go through changes physically, emotionally, spiritually, intellectually. And grace toward others around you as well.

Patricia, a former Fortune 20 Managing Director, offers her thoughts precisely on this point:

I've really lived through two Next Seasons at this point. When I initially transitioned out of my corporate role, I wanted to keep working, but in a different setting. So I took a position as a university administrator. Now a few years later, I'm moving out of fulltime work and discovering my second Next Season! Retirement isn't a "one-and-done" experience, but a series of exciting choices and transitions. My advice:

- *__Accept when it's time to move on.__ I could feel myself losing intensity toward the end of my corporate career, and I knew I needed a slower pace of life. I could have hung on a few more years, but I did what was best for me at the time.*

- *__Consider self-assessment.__ I talked with my friends and former colleagues and attended an intensive executive program de-*

signed to assist in career transitions. This helped me focus on what I really enjoy doing, as well as what I am good at.

- **Consider getting involved with your alma mater or your child's university.** *It can offer a balance between the corporate world and a not-for-profit. A university is often run more like a business, with more structure, but it also has the not-for-profit mentality where the focus is less concentrated on efficiency and the bottom line.*

- *Have realistic expectations at a not-for-profit. Your experience as a top-tier executive will be valued, but you will need to be sensitive to the organization's employees, policies, and experience. Don't expect to make changes on the first day; there will be a lot for you to learn as well. Listen before making decisions.*

- *A not-for-profit can be both rewarding and frustrating. It may not be as stressful as a corporate job, but resources are limited and the pace of decision-making can be slow.*

- **Do something that excites you when you wake up daily.** *This is a season of life where you have more flexibility, so do things that make you happy.*

- **Have days with nothing scheduled.** *With this free time, I've visited museums, gone to the movies, met up with friends, or just stayed in to read a book. Don't worry about boredom: you can counter that if and when it comes.*

- *Change your plan if it's not working. I know I have a hard time quitting something once I start, but at this point in life, I think it is more important to enjoy what you are doing. Make the most out of this Next Season in your life and every experience you choose to create.*

In our first Next Season, part of what happens is learning how to transition well, including acceptance of your new self and others. Once you are through the biggest transition—moving on from your structured corporate life—each subsequent transition becomes much easier.

Joe, a former international SVP, thought of his career in terms of seasons:

> *I've always set goals for myself: physical, mental, and career. When I accomplished everything, I wanted to in my career, I decided it was time to retire and focus on other aspects of my life. In this Next Season, I have goals as well, and because of these I don't feel unproductive. I'm still working toward something. My advice:*
>
> - ***This season of life is a great time to see the world.*** *Traveling for longer than a couple of days is now possible, and my wife and I take advantage of the opportunity, sometimes for weeks on end.*
>
> - ***After I retired, I continued to teach as an adjunct college professor.*** *Teaching can be a great way to add structure to your life and make some extra money without having the time constraints of a regular job.*
>
> - ***Resume old hobbies.*** *I used to fish when I was younger but hadn't picked up a rod in years. I took a refresher course at a local college and have loved getting back on the water.*
>
> - ***Do what you love.*** *I love golf and now I play more than the occasional game. I practice at the driving range, play with friends, and have even traveled around the world to play some of the more prestigious courses.*
>
> - ***Think outside the box and try something new.*** *I've always been fascinated by bridges, so I took an art class to learn to draw them. Now I'm planning to write a kids' book about bridges.*
>
> - ***Write down your goals to make them more tangible.*** *Try making lists like "50 Things I Want to Do in the Next 10 Years."*

- **Stay active to keep in good health.** *I go on daily walks with my wife, but I also do yard work, go get the groceries, work out, and play golf. Exercise doesn't have to be dreaded.*

- **My time is mine.** *When I was working, even Saturdays were not free. Now I'm like a 10-year-old on summer vacation! The time is mine, and I get to decide how I spend it, which has been a wonderful gift.*

The metaphor we are using here, of life's changing seasons, is thoughtfully chosen. Your first big transition out of corporate life is much like the transition from winter to spring. And spring is filled with color and possibility.

Bulbs planted last fall and in the autumns before, long forgotten, now sprout leaves and buds. Others, though nurtured and cared for meticulously, may not be as marvelous as you had expected. Hard rains and dark days lie behind the vibrant intensity of springtime colors and flowering. Other flowers appear in strange places, where the wind and birds dropped seeds you never knew about. These random flowers often take root on their own and are stunning among your otherwise carefully tended garden. And while the result may be different from what you envisioned; the truth is that it is even more beautiful.

Unexpected beauty abounds in your spring season, including the gift of the bare spots that persist despite your planting, as they enable the full radiance of the flowers to shine through.

Vivaldi captured it stunningly in his famous Four Seasons concertos, where the musical intensity varies from fast, to slow, to fast again as you navigate through four seasons of music. It is our own story as well.

The career of Mark, a retired U.S. Air force Brigadier General, mirrored Vivaldi's Four Seasons: dramatic, intense movements, punctuated by incredible crescendos and decrescendos. Mark shared the following:

After spending over 30 years in the aerospace industry, I wanted some different experiences. I went from the Air Force to taking a year off, to being president of a public company, to owning a Chick-fil-A. My mantra was "I'm not making a decision for the rest of my life. I'm just deciding what I'd like to do next." I determined I would try something for three years, and if I didn't like it, I would try something else. I have no regrets. Instead, I have stories that I hope will help others. My advice:

- **Think about what you really want to do.** *Give yourself time to process the transition, both intellectually and emotionally.*

- **Don't rush into anything.** *This is a significant life transition. Take time to assess what has made you feel fulfilled in the past, what you do well, and where there is a need. It can fit together like a puzzle.*

- **Balance contemplation with action.** *You'll know when you are ready. Don't overthink or wait for the perfect opportunity. Remember that you are not making a life-long decision. If you are interested in something, try it for a while. If you don't enjoy it, try something else.*

- **Get out of your normal routine.** *Open your mind to new possibilities. You have to make it happen. No one is going to figure out your Next Season for you.*

- **Think about how you can give back.** *Everyone has something different to contribute and offer.*

- **Don't just drift into something.** *Once you make a decision and head in a direction, opportunities will present themselves.*

- **Enjoy the flexibility.** *Time is your asset.*

Always remember that there is not just one Next Season—but many more changing seasons. Grace and acceptance are key. Some transitions we initiate, whereas others happen, whether we will them or not. And thank goodness for that!

Vicki Escarra

Previous Role: Chief Marketing Officer, Delta Airlines

Retirement Date: 2004

Next Season Passions:
- Global Not-for-Profit CEO
- Board Member
- Executive Advisor

My first Next Season

I had been with Delta Airlines for nearly 30 years and held off leaving because I wanted to support them while they navigated the emotional and organizational aftereffects of 9/11. With my Executive Advisor, I discussed transitioning into something different, ultimately leading me to a decision that changed the course of my life.

Testing the waters

Through advisory support and my network of connections, I landed on spending a year working for the Mayor of Atlanta, Georgia—supporting her rebranding efforts for the city. Following an advocacy event in the city that I had attended with her, we discussed what my Next Season might be.

She asked, "Vicki, when are you going to do something really great with your life? Something that will *really* affect people?" Her words stuck with me, and her guidance was a catalyst for my second Next Season.

A rewarding pivot

That's when I started seeking full-time not-for-profit opportunities. I had been fortunate in my career, so whatever came next didn't require a lot of money. I joined *America Second Harvest* as CEO, leading the rebranding of their nationwide food bank network as *Feeding America*, now the number-one U.S. not-for-profit. I later became CEO of *Opportunity International*, expanding my NFP impact by supporting global communities in extreme poverty, helping individuals build sustainable incomes, educate their children, and break the cycle of generational poverty.

The ups and downs of moving forward

My strong parents taught me valuable life lessons about moving forward, so I'm a pretty tough cookie! I was not blind to the challenges when I dove into these Next Seasons. One of the hardest was moving to Chicago to join *Feeding America* as CEO. I really missed family and

There are plenty of unique opportunities out there, you just have to discover which is meant to be yours. Go with what you love, and you will find it."

friends left behind in Atlanta. But I made new friends quickly with *Feeding America's* Board, wider network, and staff. I also reconnected with a high school friend, who showed me the sites. I fell in love with Chicago. These connections helped me adjust during the transition.

Balancing heart and mind

When you are deciding what to do next, my first advice is *go with your head, but also your heart*. Doing deep research on companies I considered joining, I got to know every organization, their CEO, and the Board before joining. It was important to understand the details and who I would be making big organizational decisions alongside. It also had to be something that I loved.

I suggest using a pie chart to see where your time goes: How much time are you spending with your faith? Exercising? Sleeping? Working? Nurturing relationships?

Consider where you are spending your time and where you hope to spend it in the future.

Next Seasons, new perspectives

Raised in a middle-class family, I did not realize the extent of U.S. food insecurity. Millions of Americans don't have enough to eat—mostly kids and single mothers trying to raise children while living on minimum wage, and senior citizens whose income is tapped out.

After joining *Opportunity International*, I saw astonishing poverty in Africa and India. People who have nothing but are so *gracious*—they would invite us into their homes, serve us tea, and celebrate our presence. The experience showed me how truly fortunate we are. I still had growth targets and metrics to meet. The Board's goal: operate like a for-profit, but with a heart. To sustain and grow our impact, there were global strategies to implement and cost savings to achieve.

Meaningful influence in each Season

I now share my experience and lessons learned as an executive coach and advisor. I advise NFP leaders and continue my impact in new ways, including streamlining key government programs like SNAP, unemployment benefits, and supporting environmental programs.

What's next?

My kids say I'll never stop working! I get joy from it, and it keeps me engaged. It keeps my mind fresh, especially working alongside younger professionals.

I don't know what's next, but there will be another Next Season for me! As I advise others, I seek something driven by my passions. There are unique opportunities out there—you just have to discover which is yours. *Go with what you love, and you will find it.*

12

Top 10 Lessons Learned from Leaders Post-Transition

··

A Summary of Our Client's Reflections

The following summarizes the Top 10 lessons we have observed, and our clients have shared, over our first ten years of supporting leaders in transition. The details behind each of these lessons are in the preceding chapters.

1. **Start early.**
   Begin discernment while there is still runway in your current role.

2. **Leave well.**
   How you finish/transition determines how you begin your Next Season.
   a. When it's on your terms
   b. When it's on your company's terms

3. **Manage your emotions in the early days.**
   The early days are difficult. Anticipate and plan for those. Take a Pause. It Matters.

4. **Do not rush into a "what's next."**
   You need time to detox from the pace and intensity—and the emotions that accompany separation. There will be pressure from many to commit right away to something—anything—and you yourself may feel as though you have an expiration date. It is important to give yourself some breathing space to consider what you want to do next—and for word to reach others that you are "available." Sometimes after stepping away from a major role, you need a prolonged pause while you reground yourself, focus on your personal health, wellness, life.

5. **Decide what to say yes (and no) to.**
   You have options. Be intentional in what you say "yes" to in your first, Next Season. You have lacked capacity to do things of your choosing for many, many years. Do not commit prematurely and then wish you had space to do something more interesting/different.

6. **Rely on others, and in turn be there for them**.
   Change. Business. Life. It's a team sport. Relationships are essential, and are one of the things you will miss most about leaving. Forging new ones allows you to move forward and not just cling to past friendships.

7. **Tap your amazing network.**
   Tap into it in new ways. Expand it now for future possibilities.

8. **Prioritize health and well-being.**
   If there is one statement that applies to all things in life it would be that our health is our rate-limiter for all we want to do. With good health we have a world of possibilities. Without it, we are challenged and limited on so many levels. As you enter this period of transition, there is no more important time to double-down on your health than now.

9. **Rebrand yourself and define the new you.**

   Don't assume your reputation speaks for itself. Ensure your story is well-told and your successes and goals are well-articulated. Update your professional materials, both on paper and online, and ensure you have a powerful pitch that demonstrates your value going forward. Don't talk about who you were—talk about who you want to be!

10. **Involve your spouse/partner meaningfully in the process. Prioritize family.**

    Couples experience a lot of tugs and pulls when one or both have demanding jobs. Vacations get cut short or are interrupted by conference calls or virtual meetings. Family events are missed. Relocations occur, disrupting family lives and dynamics. Spouses/partners have a strong and vested interest in "what's next" and how it may impact them.

Ben Markham

Previous Role: Vice President of Engineering, ExxonMobil Research and Engineering

Retirement Date: 2003

Next Season Passions:
· Board President & Founder, Empower Playgrounds

Called to give back

I've been very fortunate! I found what I wanted to do professionally early, using my chemical engineering degrees to build a successful career at ExxonMobil. Recognizing that I've had an incredible life, I felt a need to pay that good fortune forward after retirement.

I left the schedules and demands of the corporate world behind, and my wife and I moved to Ghana on a volunteer mission with our church. Living and serving there for a year and a half ultimately led me to find a deeply rewarding Next Season legacy as Founder of Empower Playgrounds—a humanitarian effort dedicated to improving educational opportunities for children in West Africa.

Inspiration strikes

When we began our work in rural Ghanian villages, I'll never forget sitting in a dark classroom one day—just a cement block room with a door and one window. I looked at my wife and said, *"I'm not*

> *Most people want to "do good," but may not look far enough outside of their own circle to find the right opportunity."*

sure anyone can learn anything in this environment." And she said, *"I'm sure they can't."* And that was it—that was the moment I realized I had to do something.

That same afternoon, I started drawing on the back of an envelope—playing with physics and trying to figure out how to generate a little bit of electricity. I came up with the idea of using some kind of playground equipment to harness the children's playtime energy for use in lighting their classrooms and homes. And that was the beginning of what became Empower Playgrounds.

Engaging my network

When we returned home, I reached out to some faculty friends at Brigham Young University. With the help of these educators and their engineering students, we designed a merry-go-round that used a portion of the children's play energy to generate electricity, to be stored in a portable golf cart–type battery.

The power could then be used to recharge LED lanterns that could light classrooms and be taken home by students in the evenings. As most schools didn't have playground equipment, the merry-go-rounds were a welcomed addition that served multiple purposes.

Compounded effect

The merry-go-rounds not only provide an outlet for play—an important component of learning—but also serve as a living lab for real-life science education, including a window in the merry-go-round that allows the kids to observe the generator and gear box inside. And of course, they are producing essential energy that empowers (lights their way) to further learning.

Historically, most children in rural Ghana do not make it to the high school level. But the merry-go-round–powered lanterns are influential in changing that—providing enough light for children to study after dark once they finish helping with chores at home.

The total cost of an installed system is about $10,000, which supplies 200 children with electricity for at least five years. It breaks down to about $10 per year to give a child the gift of light and learning.

Joy in action

We installed the first Empower Playgrounds merry-go-round in Ghana in 2008. Within 15 minutes, we had 60 kids on the merry-go-round jumping up and down and singing! I was so excited that first day. Seeing the children in the village literally mob the merry-go-round—they never had anything to play on before—generated excitement in me that has just continued.

Expanded impact

Since 2008, Empower Playgrounds has helped nearly 23,000 students and expanded offerings to a variety of resources with the core mission of enabling better educational opportunities. In addition to the merry-go-rounds, we now have three areas of focus: providing light, augmenting education, and promoting wellness.

For lighting, we offer a lantern-share program and a village solar project, both of which deliver safe lighting for homes and completing tasks after sundown.

To augment education, our solutions help Ghanian junior high school students pass their high school entrance exam. We have established libraries and computer labs and provide science kits and scholarships to enhance students' passion for learning and information access.

I was an engineer, and I saw a place where a little bit of engineering could make a big difference. The ideas just came, and the effort snowballed because we were listening, paying attention to what could unlock new possibilities for those who needed them."

And to promote wellness, we address some daily challenges of life in rural Ghana. Many people lack access to clean water sources, and illness and even menstruation, can keep students from attending school. We strive to remove these roadblocks by drilling boreholes that pump clean water, supplying reusable menstruation kits, and installing BioFil toilets that enhance sanitation.

Early-on we established a team on the ground in Ghana who are full partners in helping us continue to find new, meaningful ways to improve and expand educational opportunities for Ghanian children.

Being intentional

Most people want to "do good," but may not look far enough outside of their own circle to find the right opportunity. Such opportunities don't happen by accident. My advice is *go find it*—seek out that opportunity that inspires and enables leveraging your professional skills in service to others. It might be a local food pantry, or a tutoring group, or whatever it is—but just get involved and keep your eyes open for new ways to help.

> *In rural Ghana, I'm a celebrity (at 78)! I have 20,000 kids who know and happily greet me. How amazing is that?"*

I was an engineer, and I saw a place where a little bit of engineering could make a big difference. The ideas just came, and the effort snowballed because we were listening, paying attention to what could unlock new possibilities for those who needed them.

A redefined identity

In rural Ghana, I'm a celebrity (at 78)! I have 20,000 kids who know and happily greet me. How amazing is that? Since 2005, I have been to Ghana 26 times, and I'm going back soon—to recharge my own battery! It's easy to get mired down in fund-raising and other administrative challenges, but we must never forget the "why" behind our good deeds.

I was fortunate to find something that really motivates me. It's so fulfilling, the perfect progression of my professional success into a satisfying and life-changing Next Season. Sometimes I think to myself, *"Maybe the world improved just a little bit because of what I did."*

*****

Empower Playgrounds *aims to enhance the educational opportunities for children in rural Ghana. To learn more about Empower Playgrounds and how you can support the work they do, please visit* **empowerplaygrounds.org**.

13

Postlude:
Carpe Diem, Again!

....
Be choiceful in your Next Season

The transition to your Next Season starts from an unprecedented position of strength. You likely have the good fortune to be financially secure, with an established reputation, at the peak of your skills with a lifetime of experience, and many years of healthy life ahead of you. Some of you will go on to pursue further income-earning opportunities that further extend and capitalize on your incredible gifts and talents.

Regardless, it is important to seize the opportunity and be choiceful about what you do in your Next Season. Gone are the years of needing to impress certain people to get ahead. Gone are the conditional promotions/quests for approval of a boss. You are free to be incredibly intentional about how you spend your time and with whom. What a gift!

This book has been about how to make the most of this opportunity and to share the wisdom and insights of those who have made the transition to their Next Season. Every leader's situation is as varied as we are different as people, but here are important themes that have universal value:

- **This is your unique opportunity.** It will define your next phase of life. You can think it through with the confidence that you will never be better prepared and less constrained. With all your career-building years behind you, it is your unique opportunity to think about what you really would *enjoy* doing with your life going forward. You have paid your dues. Now it's time to explore and find what will give you personal joy and satisfaction.

- **Your Next Season is likely just the first of several.** Many leaders find it useful to think of multiple seasons with various themes that drive their priorities—escaping the corporate world, reconnecting with their community, becoming part of their grandchildren's lives, pursuing a lifelong passion or interest. Themes like these can impact where and how you live and may require deeper, longer-range consideration.

- **Start the transition before you retire.** It is never easy to find the time in your busy schedule, but thinking this through with your spouse/partner, before you actually retire, is a great way to welcome this major transition into your lives as a shared endeavor. It will make the change much less stressful if it becomes a part of the continuum of your lives. In addition, many of the contacts/arrangements you will need to make may be unfamiliar and will take time to establish. It is really helpful if there is minimal "dead space" between your corporate life and the activities of your Next Season. Take that trip of a lifetime— to sit back, enjoy what you have achieved as you celebrate your new freedom.

- **Think about the balance between your commitments and unstructured time.** This is particularly important regarding your family. In your Next Season, your unstructured time itself becomes an important commitment. Particularly with grandchildren—their needs, and your opportunity to be an intimate participant in their lives, is very often unscripted— and once lost, cannot be retrieved.

- **You are entering unknown territory.** The opportunities that you imagine at the outset often are overtaken by things you did not at all anticipate. A joy of this period in your life is having the flexibility to take on things you never thought of!

- **Pay attention to your health.** This is obvious, but it bears repeating: your health determines the quality of your Next Season more than any other factor. You now have the opportunity to dedicate time to regular exercise. So go for it—but don't be too ambitious. It is better to have a sensible program and stick to it.

- **Not investing in your health is cumulative.** This is insidious, sneaking up on you. There doesn't seem to be much difference in your sixties, but the difference in what you are able to do after age 70 becomes dramatic— and for a leader who is contemplating retirement in their early sixties, that difference is huge.

- **Continue to learn.** A colleague who is approaching 90 and is still very active, with a wide circle of influence, advises that "the secret of a long and happy life is to remain invested in the future."

- **Stay open, remain relevant.** The increasing pace in the evolution of knowledge provides a fascinating opportunity to grasp ideas which have never been possible, and you need to do so to stay relevant.

- **Don't get trapped by administrative burden.** Now is the time to focus on things that exercise your mind and body and nurture your soul. Keep it simple and engage assistance with the administrative duties.

- **Be a good partner—it's worth your weight in gold.** In many respects this is now your companion's time. After many years in which priorities may have been secondary to the demands of your career, this is the time when you can share the opportunity of this Next Season together (there is a debt to be paid!).

Finally, we surveyed our clients about what surprised them about the transition to their Next Season. We heard these common themes:

- **How well it had gone**—given the fear that many expressed at the outset.

- **How difficult the idea of retirement is** after a lifelong career and how powerful it is to view it as an opportunity.

- **The need to become very good at self-initiation.** One of the realities of your Next Season is that if you don't do it, it likely won't get done!

We wish you well on your journey. Have faith. And recall . . .

To everything there is a season,
and a time to every purpose under heaven.

The following "**Your Next Season Tools**"
are excerpts from the MyNextSeason
company's Workbook and advisory tools.
They are intended to help you begin thinking
about and preparing for your Next Season.

Your Next Season Tools

Discerning Your Next Season

We have found that planning your Next Season is well served by first naming the parameters that define the preferences, or in some cases, non-negotiables to incorporate/work around as you plan your next season.

Section 1—Parameters

1. **Geography**

   a. Do you have existing commitments that commit you geographically?

   b. What are your early thoughts about where you'd like to live all or some of the time?

2. **Financial**

   a. Are there financial concerns or considerations that impact how you want to spend your Next Season? For example, do you need/wish to continue to earn an income?

   b. Are there investments you have committed to, or that are forthcoming of a significant nature, that you will want to/need to honor in your next season?

3. **Medical**

   a. Are there any personal or family medical concerns or considerations that impact your plans or define where you wish to receive medical care?

   b. Are there any personal objectives you have for yourself physically that will impact your time/priorities after your transition?

   c. Where/with whom will you ensure your health/well-being/medical needs, are met in your next season?

4. **Commitments You Bring with You**

   a. Are there any individuals, causes, organizations, or people to whom you feel an obligation or desire to be engaged with/supportive of in your Next Season? Approximately how much time does fulfilling these require?

5. **Time**

   As you consider how you might spend time after you leave your current job, list things you have always imagined yourself doing (for example, playing golf, speaking to audiences on favorite topics, reading three newspapers every morning, volunteering, reading novels, joining a gym, traveling, writing a book, taking classes, learning a language, working, spending time with grandchildren).

6. **Your Definition of Success**

   a. Sitting here today, describe what "success" looks like to you on the other side of this career transition.

   b. Describe any particular concerns you have about the transition.

7. **Caring for Others**

   Do you have obligations or caregiving responsibilities that impact how or where you will spend your Next Season?

Section 2—The Highlights

Please complete the following sentences.

1. **I love**

2. **I am happiest when**

3. **The following things have been the highlights of:**

   - My past year
   - My past decade
   - My most recent job
   - My career
   - My community life
   - My marriage/partnership
   - My children/grandchildren
   - My friendships

4. **Work accomplishments I am the most proud of:**

5. **Non-work accomplishments I am the most proud of:**

6. A good day for me is one in which (*check all that apply*):

☐ I have a schedule for the day	☐ I have no schedule for the day
☐ I am highly productive	☐ I can relax and not feel guilty
☐ I organize something	☐ I am invited and just have to show up
☐ I can be creative	☐ I can accomplish something
☐ I am intellectually stimulated	☐ I do things that don't require me to think too much
☐ I socialize with people	☐ I am alone or in the company of my spouse
☐ I am athletic	☐ I do nothing too strenuous
☐ I volunteer/help others	☐ I can work on my own things
☐ I see/do new things	☐ I engage in familiar tasks/activities
☐ I travel	☐ I am at home
☐ I solve problems	☐ I am not burdened with problems/issues
☐ I have extended time with children/grandchildren	☐ I can enjoy discrete visits with my children/grandchildren
☐ I win in golf, tennis, or some other sporting event	☐ I enjoy time with family/friends playing/watching golf, tennis, or some sporting event.

Section 3—The Lowlights

Create your personal "What Bugs Me" list.

1. What have been the lowlights of:

    a. My past year

    b. My most recent job

    c. My career

    d. My community life

    e. My marriage/partnership

Section 4—Legacy Matters

1. **Let's say your old college friend is reading an update on graduates prior to attending your 50th college reunion. He is now reading what the reporter wrote about you. Complete your story beginning with the sentence . . .**

   After leaving a highly successful career at X company, <your name>
   _____ *. . . During that time, <your name> also*
   _____ *. . . A close friend of <your name> said*
   _____ *. . . about him/her . . .*
   You will most often find <your name> doing
   _____ *. . .*

2. **What "things" would you most like to impact in your lifetime?**

   a. Are there any "causes" that you feel especially drawn to?

   b. Are there any not-for-profit organizations you would like to become more active with?

   c. Is there anything on your "What Bugs Me" list that you would be excited to tackle/change/fix?

3. **How do you wish your children/grandchildren to remember you? How will they come to know your life stories, experiences, accomplishments?**

Section 5—Things You Hope to Do Post-Transition

Check all that apply.

- ☐ Have more leisure time
- ☐ Work out regularly
- ☐ Travel
- ☐ Golf/tennis/other sports
- ☐ Engage in extreme physical adventures
- ☐ Volunteer (please indicate if you have specific ideas about with whom)
- ☐ Continue with a corporate career
- ☐ Start own company
- ☐ Consult/advise
- ☐ Take classes, earn degree
- ☐ Teach
- ☐ Lecture/speaking opportunities
- ☐ Mentor/tutor young people
- ☐ Be outdoors more
- ☐ Cook (more often)
- ☐ Entertain friends (more often)
- ☐ Learn new language

- ☐ Board service
  - o Publicly traded company
  - o Small/mid-size but established
  - o Startup
  - o Not-for-profit
  - o Private Equity/VC
- ☐ Not-for-Profit
  - o Board Member
  - o Management
  - o Volunteer
  - o Special Projects
- ☐ Paint/draw
- ☐ Garden
- ☐ Spend (more) time with children/grandchildren
- ☐ Coach/train
- ☐ Write
- ☐ Photography
- ☐ Master new skill
- ☐ Work with my hands
- ☐ Be a caregiver to others
- ☐ Church/synagogue work
- ☐ Deepen my faith
- ☐ Other...

Section 6—Your Marriage/Partnership

As retiring executives, we need to understand our spouse/partner's goals and how we can help them, while simultaneously achieving our own goals—those that we share with our spouse/partner and others that nurture healthy independence.

Below are some questions for you to work through individually and then as a couple.

1. **What are your respective goals/dreams for your next season?**

2. **How can you support one another in the achievement of those goals?**

3. **How would you describe the current state of your marriage partnership?**

   - We operate mostly in parallel and connect occasionally as needed.
   - We operate mostly in parallel, because that's what the job has required of us, but we connect whenever we can and enjoy that time together.
   - We operate well, both independently and together—and look forward to having more together time.
   - We operate mostly as a team and expect that to continue into the future.
   - We operate mostly as a team and look forward to more individual exploration in retirement.
   - Other (please elaborate).

4. **What about your response to #1 would you like to keep... and what, if anything, would you like to change.**

5. **What would make this the very best season of your marriage/partnership?**

Section 7—Spouse/Partner's Input

(This section is to be completed by your spouse/partner only.)

1. **You have been asked to submit (anonymously) responses to the following questions about your spouse/partner:**
    a. Who is this person at the core?

    b. What does he/she stand for?

    c. What makes him/her tick?

    d. When is he/she the happiest?

    e. What frustrates him/her?

    f. Of what is he/she proudest in life? (either personal or work)

2. **What hopes and concerns do you have about your spouse's/ partner's "retirement"?**

3. **Describe your perfect "day in the life" —post-transition—for you and your spouse/partner.**

Section 7—Working Through Your PARTNER Framework

Below is a framework to guide the conversation with your spouse/partner as you assemble a shared vision and plan for your Next Season. It is helpful to work through the framework independently first, and then discuss it together as you pull together a shared plan.

Priorities	What are your individual priorities for this Next Season? What are your priorities as a couple? Write your top 10 list, both individually and as a couple.
Alternatives	You have considered what you might do in this next phase of your life. What are your ideas? How you will spend your time? Where will you live? To what will you dedicate your time and resources?

Realities	What current realities/concerns do you have as you enter your Next Season?
	    What realities must you navigate as you make your plans? Are there constraints you must work with, like aging parents or health concerns? Or that you want to work with, like proximity to children or not-for-profits you have committed to?
	    Note: Do not rush through this phase. It is important to understand one another's concerns entering this phase—and to openly acknowledge variables that enable or constrain your options.

Togetherness	Some things you will want to do together, whereas other activities you will opt to pursue independently. What activities do you hope to share?
Non-togetherness	Likewise, what do you see yourselves doing independently? *Note: Healthy independence is extremely important in this phase of life. You have each carved independent paths, and you need to honor those desires and commitments as well as adding new ones together.*
Events	What actions or next steps do you need to take in light of what you've discussed/agreed to here?
Revisiting Our Plan	When will you revisit what you've discussed/agreed to here to see if adjustments need to be made?

1. My priorities in this Next Season are
2. What I love
3. Criteria for what I want to do in my Next Season
4. What I am positively *not* interested in doing
5. Some possibilities given my current thinking
6. What I would like to try (first) in the next 3 to 6 months

---

Example: "Joseph's" Next Season Framework

Joseph's Priorities

1. Regain health
2. Reconnect with my daughters
3. Do something that is helpful to others (e.g., help build homes or distribute food)
4. Improve my golf game
5. Reconnect with college friends through alumni network

What Joseph Loves

1. Being with others—I do not enjoy being alone
2. Working with my hands; I love to build things or do physical things while interacting with people
3. Playing golf

Criteria for What to Do in Next Season

1. Use my dormant skills in woodworking/building things
2. Allow time to exercise, spend time with family, and give back
3. Connect often with other people
4. Enjoy my coffee every morning

Things Not Interested In

1. Anything that creates stress
2. Working in isolation
3. Anything that precludes my being able to play golf a couple of times per week

Possibilities

1. Survey local needs for building/construction assistance (e.g., Habitat for Humanity)
2. Find a regular golf group that plays at my level
3. Hire a personal trainer to pull together an exercise routine that works with my schedule and physical condition

Acknowledgments

WHAT A GIFT IT HAS BEEN to have such an amazing team of colleagues to journey the past 10 years with! Without them, we could not have served thousands of clients making important, and often tender, career transitions.

Specifically, we recognize and thank: Amy Baldwin, Amy Lynn Banek, Deborah Bell, Frank Berardi, Terry Bickham, Bill Bloom, Alan Booth, Charles Bowman, Austin Braksick, Lauren Brand, Jean Brinkmann, Jessica Broaders, Wayne Cafran, Angelique Carbo, Leanne Caret, Vanessa Castagna, Scott Coolidge, Dr. Jennifer Daley, Sharon Daley, Debbie Dellinger, Edana Desatnick, Carolyn Dewing-Hommes, Richard Downen, Christine Eosco, Vicki Escarra, Trevor Fetter, Christine Furstoss, Sharon Ingles Fury, Maggie Gervasi, Marty Gervasi, Andrew Gray, Jeannie Hodes, Gina Hutchins, Bill Innes, Alan Kelly, Natalie Kronzer, John Landry, Rani Lange, Deirdre Latour, Michael LeRoy, Peter Lichtenthal, Anna Linsz, Vanessa Lo, Bill Lorenz, Katie Morgan, Shamla Naidoo, George Peterson, Vipin Ramani, Sharon Ritchey, Steve Schaick, Al Schnur, Mike Sharp, Evan Smith, Monica Tarr, Sara Tate, Truett Tate, Linda Whitley Taylor, John Thiel, Geri Thomas, Kathryn Trice, Burnet Tucker, Danielle Vigueria, Jean Wallace, Hilary Ware, Dr. Kenneth Weeks, Dr. John Whyte, Rhiannon Williams, Paul Wirth, Peter Wong, Amy Woods Brinkley, and Shannon Wright.

We are deeply grateful to those who allowed us to share their stories in this book. By conveying your personal experiences, you helped in two important ways. First, you helped bring our concepts to life in relatable ways. And second, your stories bring comfort and comradery to our readers, by showing that they are not alone in their experiences, challenges, and emotions. Readers can share your optimism and hope while navigating similar uncertainties. Thank you for your gift of openness and vulnerability.

We also thank our early reviewers and others who offered valuable feedback, insights, and endorsements: Lucien Alziari, Rob Arning, Amy Lynn Banek, Frank Berardi, Doria Camaraza, Rob Cañizares, Leanne Caret, Vanessa Castagna, Connie Chartrand,

David Churchill, David Clair, Titi Cole, Neil Cotty, Sharon Daley, Mike D'Ambrose, Tom DiDonato, Richard Downen, Elise Eberwein, Laura Ellsworth, Vicki Escarra, Trevor Fetter, Kim Tillotson Fleming, Michael Fraccaro, Ed Galante, Marty Gervasi, Vicki Henn, Raanan Horowitz, Edward A. Kangas, Alan & Carol Kelly, Clark Kinlin, Tim McMahon, Glenda McNeal, Brian McNeill, Adel Melek, Dee Mellor, AP Mery, Dionne Wallace Oakley, Rebecca O'Toole, Susan P. Peters, Joe Price, Michael Ramage, David Robinson, Jack Ryan, Eva Sage-Gavin, Ed Sannini, Mike Sharp, Gary Sheffer, Kevin Silva, David Simms, Andrea Smith, Dr. Julie M. Smith, Anne Steele, John Thiel, Burnet Tucker, Jim Unruh, and Dr. Jonathan Lee Walton. Your wisdom made the final version even stronger!

Deep appreciation for our editor Fred Schroyer, senior writer Jeannie Hodes, graphic designer Jim Scattaregia, and project manager Rhiannon Williams, whose efforts helped us take a draft to a published book.

Finally, nothing we do is possible without the unwavering love and support of our spouses Matt Braksick and Becky Linsz. Your love and encouragement to pursue our vision with MyNextSeason enabled our dream to become a reality. And to our children and grandchildren: each of you fills our cups, enriching all that we do. Hugs to our Braksick family—Anna, Austin, Madeleine, Payton, Reagan, Sydney, and Vince; and to our Linsz family—Anna, Ashley, Chris, Ellie, and Hannah.

Your Authors

Leslie Wilk Braksick, Ph.D.

A VETERAN EXECUTIVE, entrepreneur, CEO coach, board member, and author, Leslie co-leads MyNextSeason, drawing on decades of expertise as an advisor to senior corporate leaders, bringing deep understanding around the often complex and fragile transitions out of dominating careers. Prior to launching MyNextSeason, Leslie co-founded the management consultancy Continuous Learning Group, Inc. which specializes in strategy execution for the Fortune 500. Leslie led and grew the firm as its Chairman and President/ CEO while consulting as an Executive Advisor to its seniormost clients. Leslie was recently honored with the OBM Network Lifetime Achievement Award, given to individuals who have fundamentally advanced the understanding or application of behavioral principles in organizational settings. A respected thought leader in her field, her works on executive leadership and transition are used in graduate programs and corporations around the world. She recently co-authored *Preparing CEOs for Success: Insights from CEOs and Directors*, revealing important shifts in best preparing and onboarding C-suite Executives. Her earliest book, *Unlock Behavior, Unleash Profits* made WSJ's Business Best Seller list.

Leslie currently serves on the Board of Children's Hospital of Pittsburgh, is an Emeritus Board Member of the Princeton Theological Seminary and a founding board member of the Eradicate Hate Global Summit. She holds a Ph.D. in Applied Behavioral Science, an M.A. in Industrial Psychology, both from Western Michigan University, and a Master's degree in Public Health from Johns Hopkins University.

Leslie and husband Matthew have been married for over 33 years and are blessed by adult children Austin (Anna), Madeleine (Vince), and three precious granddaughters. A full biography is available at lesliebraksick.com

Mark D. Linsz

MARK LINSZ is Co-Founder and Senior Managing Partner of MyNextSeason. Leveraging his personal insights gained from his own transition, he is a caring Advisor who encourages clients to take the time they need to develop a purposeful Next Season plan. He applies his encouraging and candid approach to demystify the perceived complexities of transition and provide reassurance that each person's unique skills will remain relevant and valuable for years to come.

Prior to starting MyNextSeason, Mark spent more than two decades at Bank of America, most notably steering the company safely as Corporate Treasurer for four years during the worst of the financial crisis. In that role, Mark managed the bank's $2T balance sheet and raised over $50B of capital while ensuring funding and liquidity of all the bank's entities. While at Bank of America, Mark also served as CFO Risk Executive, Capital Markets Risk Executive, and Chief Risk Officer for Europe, Middle East, Africa, and Asia. Throughout his career, Mark has worked internationally and led global teams in Chicago, New York, Charlotte, London, and Hong Kong.

Mark is regularly sought out for his expertise in financial services and managing global teams, and he applies that expertise as a board member. He currently serves on the board of CNL Strategic Capital and a Falfurrias Capital portfolio company board. He has served on the board of directors for BlackRock, the Depository Trust & Clearing Corporation (DTCC), and Corporate Capital Trust II. Mark is currently on the board of African Bible Colleges and he is a founding board member of Freedom Communities, an organization working to revive the west side of Charlotte, NC.

Mark has been married to his wife, Becky, for over 30 years and is the father of Ashley, Anna, and Ellie.

About MyNextSeason

MYNEXTSEASON was co-founded in 2014 by Dr. Leslie Braksick and Mark Linsz, two seasoned executives who envisioned providing a bridge for retiring leaders as they transition—from corporate careers oriented to *productivity*, to Next Seasons anchored in *purpose*. MyNextSeason is unlike any other firm out there, with three primary differentiators:

1. **Our Advisors.** All are former senior leaders of major companies and organizations, who themselves transitioned and found joy and fulfillment in their Next Season. Visit https://mynextseason. com/about-us/ to meet the dozens of advisors who support our clients by sharing their wisdom, experience, insights, connections, and deeply caring approach.

2. **Our Process.** We customize every client engagement to meet their unique needs, circumstances, and goals. Success is determined by our client's achievement of their goals, not by us. Whether it's improving their skills/profile for future board service, mentoring/ teaching/helping others in their discipline, focusing on health improvement, or simply dialing-back life's intensity to focus on relationships and other priorities, our team surrounds each client with fit-for-purpose support, tools (resume, bio, LinkedIn profile, etc.) and connections needed for them to reveal/realize their Next Season. We leave nothing to chance.

3. **Our Tools**. Clients are guided through a thoughtful, proprietary Workbook and access our extensive online resource library with videos and guidance to discern and develop their transition priorities/plan, on topics like joining boards, college teaching, leading non-profits, PE, consulting, strong interests, etc.

At the company level, MyNextSeason partners with Chief Human Resource Officers to help companies customize support of their leaders in the last decade (or so) of their careers. The most visionary HR leaders clearly see the linkage between professional development, retention, and early transition planning—and thus do the #1 thing that thousands of clients tell us they wish they had done: *start planning early.*

Universally, clients wish they had started long before the transition was either somewhere on the horizon or actually in progress. MyNextSeason is crafting highly innovative, customized executive-development programs that grow leaders, shake hands with career planning, and eventually provide transition support. This allows clients to broaden their skills, explore interests that mutually benefit both company and leader while they are still in their role, sample potential interests for their Next Season, finish their career well, and transition well to their successor.

Some companies lack the luxury of early planning, and thus seek help for retiring leaders. Other firms are concerned with smoothing exits that happen earlier than anticipated/desired by the impacted leader. Still other companies encounter a business strategy that necessitates transitioning large numbers of people with little notice.

MyNextSeason understands and embraces each unique circumstance and works with HR to create fit-for-purpose solutions for both company and individuals. Additionally, our client companies experience huge retention benefits when those who remain see their coworkers so deeply respected and actively cared for, even at the sunset of their careers.

We help you live your company's values around people—even in the final phases of their distinguished careers. Visit https:// mynextseason.com/, email us at info@mynextseason.com, or call 412-802-9196. We are excited to help!

Made in the USA
Middletown, DE
31 October 2024

63667051R00106